HOW THE CHURCH GROWS

HOW
THE CHURCH
GROWS

ROY A. BURKHART

WITH A FOREWORD BY

HENRY R. LUCE

PUBLISHERS
HARPER & BROTHERS
NEW YORK AND LONDON

HOW THE CHURCH GROWS

To

DR. WILLIAM H. BODDY

for the richness of his teaching

To

THE STAFF AND MEMBERS OF

THE FIRST COMMUNITY CHURCH

for all they have taught me

To

MY FAMILY

for their love and understanding

CONTENTS

FOREWORD ✒︎

NO ONE today is surprised to be told that about one-half of the people of America do not belong to any church or synagogue. But a good many people, even among those who have read history, seem astonished to learn that that was always the case. We have got used to the notion that in the "modern" world, church-going is a minority habit. We have forgotten that in this country it always was.

There is also the notion that whereas the Roman Catholic Church is on the increase, there has been a long downward trend in Protestant church membership. The Roman Catholic Church *is* increasing; and so, also, are the Protestant churches.

There are today some 45,000,000 Protestant church members in the United States—substantially more than ever before. *And* Protestants today add up to a higher percentage of our total population than at any time in American history. Moreover, there is much confirming evidence of vitality in many sectors of Protestantism. The recent drive for $135,000,000 for postwar reconstruction funds is significant not only for the size of the amount but, much more strikingly, because in thousands of congregations giving to the reconstruction funds seems to have been the most cheerful, the most deeply consecrated giving which has been experienced in many a year.

And yet, even when the ignorance of most of our intelligentsia on the subject of Protestantism is duly corrected, is it not still a fact that Protestant Christianity is simply not the moral and social power which it once was in our land? Yes—something of that sort would certainly appear to be a fact. And is it not true that the dominant thought and feeling in America is secular rather than religious? Yes—surely, the last four or five decades have been marked by the triumph of secularism— a triumph entailing and foretelling universal catastrophe.

Thus, despite the statistics cited, most thoughtful people would probably agree that modern American society as a whole is, in fact, far more secular and far less religious than it was at any other period. Indeed, statistics do not controvert this reasonable assumption. There has been some recent increase in Protestant giving *but* the percentage of income which even the contemporary church member gives to church activities is far less than it was at the turn of the century. And it is just in the last few years that the American people as a whole have crossed an interesting statistical divide: they are now spending more for cosmetics, more for liquor, more for tobacco—more for each of these things—than for *all* charitable activities, religious and secular combined.

More people are members of Protestant churches today than ever before—but Protestant Christianity no longer stands out as the chief guide and standard of private and public morality. Christianity, with all its natural exfoliation in moral standards and in loving-kindness, has ceased to be the characteristic ideal of American life. Its place has been taken by a secularism some- times redeemed by a Christian inheritance, which is often liberal and humane, but which is ultimately death to the soul of man.

Everyone who has a concern for the Christian Gospel has pondered this situation which, in a word, might be called the accelerating de-Christianization of America. Why has it hap- pened?

The historian will give an answer in terms of the infinitely complex pattern of history. The individual Christian, pastor or layman, will know that it is because individual Christians have failed in faith and fidelity. But whatever else may be involved, it is now becoming clear that the decline in the effective influence of Christianity on contempory civilization is a decline in the effectiveness of the Church. And in America that means the decline in the effectiveness of the Protestant church or churches.

There is a growing determination today, beginning with private individual devotion to the Gospel, that the course of American history should now be radically changed: that there should be a decrease in the authority which secularism wields over the thought and feeling and imagination of America; that there should be an increase in the authority of the Nazarene and His Eternal Gospel over our social, as well as our private, thinking and living. "The liberty wherewith Christ hath made us free—" that liberty must once again inspire and discipline the general freedom of man on which all Americans, in so far as they are true Americans, are religiously united.

But how is so vast a historical operation to be accomplished? The Christian knows that it is not by human contriving or human effort alone that history can be righteously fashioned. "Except the Lord build the house, they labor in vain that build it."

Nevertheless, the Christian must be up and doing. He must be busy not only with the perilous pilgrim's progress of his own soul—he must be busy, too, to invite, if not to achieve, the Kingdom of God on earth. On what field, in what group, will he act? Wherever else he acts, whatever else he does, his first business is the Church.

And what shall be done about the Church—and how? That is perhaps the most difficult program for Protestants as a whole.

I would go far beyond the decent bounds of a foreword if I were even to try to sketch the depth and breadth of the Protestant problem with respect to the fact and the idea of the Church of God.

But there is one thing which every literate Protestant can do to advance the cause of Christ's Church in America today: he can begin to think about it seriously. And there is no better way to begin to do that than to read this book.

Most people who have been concerned for the Church are well aware of the great vitality in the Community Church idea. Most of those who know about the Community Church idea have heard something of the First Community Church of Columbus, Ohio. In this book I have met for the first time the pastor of that famous church; and meeting Dr. Roy A. Burkhart has been a lively and heartening experience. For Dr. Burkhart is a true church-builder. In every page there breathes the love of the builder for his task. The reader begins with the vision—which is the beginning of all creative effort. And when the book is finished, the reader has learned how each and every one of the creative impulses and skills of man can be used in the building of God's Church, and purified and strengthened for individual and social purposes through the spirit of the creative Church.

The thoughtful reader may often feel that this book raises ultimate questions which it does not answer. It has the limitation, as well as the strength and charm, of being very American and very contemporary. But its outstanding achievement, to this reader at least, is that it overcomes many a doubt and fear and carries the sure conviction that the Church of God, eternal in the heavens, can be built, *is* being built here, now.

Henry R. Luce

PREFACE ∽∽∽

EVERYTHING we hold dear and precious is tied
up in the Church and its ministry. If persons are to become
living spirits, rather than human vegetables, the Church must
give full guidance to spiritual growth. If individuals are to
be free from the paganism of ego worship so that they may
grow into the will of God and the love of all men, the contemporary Church must grow into the True Church.

In spite of the 14,845 Catholic churches, 4,560 Jewish syna-
gogues, and 212,336 Protestant churches (according to the
1943-44 compilation of the Year Book of American Churches)
and the twenty million sermons and religious addresses given
each year, the church—in the words of Reinhold Niebuhr of
Union Theological Seminary—"becomes increasingly irrelevant
in the secular world." Despite all that God achieves through
the Church, locally and over the world, the contemporary
institution is being shaped by the world rather than shaping it.
The sins of individuals and groups and nations finally culmi-
nated in one generation in the second World War, with the
so-called Christian nations outdoing the enemy nations in
the mass slaughter of millions.

To feel the competition between local units and national
forces of the contemporary Church; to sense the growth of the
paganisms; to see the symptoms of a sick civilization portray
with increasing evidence the failure of individuals and groups
to grow in spirit and to know and love and live by the divine
will for the good of all, is a concern on the hearts of many.

I grew up in a Christian home, was superintendent of a

Sunday school in a little rural Mennonite church when I was sixteen; served as a volunteer superintendent of a Sunday school in a town and as youth director in a city and in a suburb. For three years I was national youth director of a denomination and for eight years served on the staff of a mighty fellowship of forty-one Protestant denominations. Now for twelve years I have had the rare privilege of sharing with children, youth, men and women in growing into a vital unit of the Church. In these years I have had close fellowship with many ministers and laymen—youth and adult—who live with the pain of longing for the True Church and with visions of that Church waiting to come into being.

In 1940 I tried to put down a story of the True Church; another draft was made again in 1943. These were put aside, and this is another effort which I offer to the reader, not with the feeling that it is all I would have it be, but with the prayer that it will help others in their consecration to fashion, with the Divine, the True Church in this day. Some readers may note that I have invented a new concept, the True Church, and have given it further such a dignified status as justifies its printing in capitals. By the True Church I understand an ideal institution, required indeed by the Gospel teaching, but only imperfectly realized by all our actual ecclesiastical organizations, my own church unhappily included. In referring to these existing institutions I am following the practice general in the publishing trade of using lower case initial letters.

My debt to others is beyond my words to express. To all those through the centuries who envisioned and lived the True Church; to my teachers, fellow ministers, and to writers without number; to the staff and members of the church in which I am permitted to minister; to Mrs. Marjorie Watson, who gave hours to take the broken words of the author and make them live with meaning for the reader; to John B. Chambers of Harper and Brothers, who shared with me the first thought of the book, and gave his mind in loving consecration to its writing and in love insisted on a number of rewritings; to Miss Rosemary Weimer, my secretary, for hours of assistance, and to Mrs. Dorothy West for taking the initial dictation and doing the final typing, there are no words adequate to express gratitude. In so far as the book helps in bringing the True-Church-to-be in this generation and in the future, those with me will share the gratitude to Him in Whom we live and move and have our being.

ROY A. BURKHART

February 15, 1947

ENVISIONING THE TRUE CHURCH

ON HILLS and in valleys, in hamlets and towns, in urban centers and great cities, there are buildings that have been dedicated to worship. Rising from many of them are steeples pointing heavenward and over scores of them are crosses marking the skyline. Most of them are simple, rectangular buildings with one room; others have a sanctuary with additional rooms for study and social activities; and a few are exquisite Gothic structures that cost millions of dollars to build. We call them churches, but they are not the Church. They are made of stone, brick, mortar and wood. They are material. They are sacred places rather than consecrated relationships. They stand on hallowed ground, but they are not spiritual. They are temporal, not eternal. These are not the Church! The Church is spiritual. In it heaven and earth meet. There the highlands of God join the lowlands of man. It is God's greatest gift added to man's fullest growth. It is man alone or in fellowship, with God alive in his soul and with the power to call to life the divine in others. The Church, visible and invisible, is the hope of the world.

I

We find ourselves today facing a paganism as violent as that which confronted the early Church. No language can describe our situation more accurately than does Paul in the first chapter to the Romans: "Filled with all manner of wickedness, depravity, lost viciousness; filled to the brim with envy, murder, quarrels, intrigues, and malignity—slanderers, defamers, loathed by God, outrageous, haughty, boastful, inventive and evil; disobedient to parent, devoid of conscience, false to their word, callous, merciless."

These are the evils that blight the soul and block its growth. These are the outer tyrannies that rob the soul of its inner sovereignty. The forces of collective violence differ from those in the days of the Roman Empire in that a state with the modern implements of war can control millions. Winston Churchill, referring to the English pilots during the war, said that "never had so many owed so much to so few." We might also say that never have so many been at the mercy of so few.

When we dropped the first atomic bomb, *Time* magazine published these words:

The race has been won, the weapon had been used by those upon whom civilization could best hope to depend; but the demonstration of power against living creatures instead of dead matter created a bottomless wound in the living consciousness of the race . . . when the bomb split open the universe . . . It revealed the simplest, commonest and most neglected and most important of facts; that each man is eternally and above all else responsible for his own soul, and in the terrible words of the psalmist, "No man may deliver his brother nor make arguments against his God."[1]

This is a piercing comment on our moral dilemma. Why should we descend to such levels of moral debauchery? Why should sins that blight the soul and prevent the growth of God's sovereignty in the soul become the behavior of millions in a country which professes to be Christian? Why should dependency on human authority and on earth-bound resources

[1] *Time,* August 20, 1945.

grow so great? Why should millions abandon the search for freedom of the soul and submit to regimentation of life and spirit? Why the increase of delinquency? Why the degeneracy that means the loss of moral certainty; the almost universal worship of money, sex, power and self; the decline of physical and mental health?

Does the answer to these questions lie partly with the growth of our sensate culture, partly with materialistic science that is paraded as our savior, partly with the assumption that progress is automatic? Or, is it that individuals of each generation forget the absolute necessity of finding within their own souls the complete sovereignty of God so that a free way of life naturally results and is insured?

Science is not enough. Paganism can use science for destructive aims. Education is not sufficient. Evil leaders can mobilize disciplined minds to evil ends, as did dictators of the past. Our only salvation lies in spiritual values and in the open dedication of our lives to their pursuit.

The contemporary Church is made up of millions of people who, like Joseph of Arimathea, are disciples secretly with half-hearted loyalty. It is made up of millions who want the Kingdom of God but who do not want it first. With these millions the love of God follows second to love of power, money, security and pleasure. The contemporary Church has a large majority of people who hold in their hearts the deep conviction that there is something greater in life than they are, which they call God. They contemplate with horror a world that would rob them of the freedom of worship, and yet they do not give their whole-hearted loyalty to God. They try to walk in the ways of Christ, they want his approval; in times of disappointment and sorrow they lean upon the great assurances that Christ gave. Their hearts believe in the God of love and mercy Whom Christ revealed. But never do they fully and enthusiastically declare to the world, "I am on His side, I acknowledge my debt to Him and I will do my share in making His spirit and His purpose regnant in human society."

If all the half loyalty and the secret discipleship and the lukewarm fealty that are accorded to God were suddenly to flame into fiery, zealous devotion, this generation would save an imperiled civilization. Less and less place has the world today for secret and divided loyalties. A communist will sacrifice to uphold the preachments of the communist creed and will boast his faith on the street corner. Every anti-Christian dogma is demanding of its followers wholehearted, one-directional devotion, loyalty sincerely and bravely proclaimed. Least of all times in history can we today afford a religious faith that is vague and undefined, a surreptitious lip service, a shrewd admixture of idealism and worldly astuteness, that cautiously seeks to gain heaven without losing hold of earth.

II

What are the qualities of the True Church? It is a fellowship of those who find union with God within themselves and with one another, and who bring the reality of God to all their living, day by day, to fulfill His purpose. They are a band bound by the love of God and love of their fellow men, resolutely entering all arenas of social, political and economic life—to challenge, resist, fight and finally overcome the forces of injustice, exploitation, discrimination and violence. The True Church is made up of those who share the common conviction that now is the time when the word of the Eternal must be spoken and the will of God must become the universal will by which they live for the good of all.

The True Church has a meeting place where people grow in their ability to seek and to know God; where they grow in union with God through worship, meditation, study; where they grow in the skills of witnessing to others so that they, too, may find God and His purpose for their lives. Wherever these members go, wherever they are, loving and living and doing the will of God, there the True Church is.

The True Church is a fellowship of all those who love God, seeking to grow through Christ and through all other manifestations of the Divine into the fullest awareness of God. It is a fellowship of those dedicated to helping everyone from the youngest to the oldest to fulfill his divine destiny. To each individual it holds out a workaday guide to a divine goal: to live as the earthly incarnation of God; to join, if possible, with another in a love that spans all of earthly life; to bring new life into the world and guide it into the fullest awareness of God.

The True Church is the power and the beauty by which all aspects of living become hallowed. It is the motive for the saint, the guide to the seer, the principle for the scientist, the mother of the best in the past and the father of the future waiting to be born. Within the True Church is the heart of compassion which feeds the hungry and strengthens the weak. It encompasses the mercy that heals and the love that banishes all hate, bringing the spirit of brotherhood into all the relations of men, until every human breach is healed and every difference canceled. The True Church is the light that shows all men the way of freedom.

Wherever there is a beloved community of those who seek together the whole truth and live it in love, there also is the True Church. Its creed is as comprehensive as the teachings of Christ and as all-inclusive as the love of God. It sanctions freedom for all forms of religious expression. It is a Church of, by and for those who make it up, constantly sensitive both to the Holy Spirit and to the needs of men locally and over the world. It seeks not to bring the neighborhood within its four walls, but to create the beloved community in the neighborhood. It loses itself in ministry to the spiritual needs of all, regardless of race, color or creed, and the heart of its ministry is to free men and to keep them free to seek first the Kingdom of God.

The primary concern of the True Church is to find the truth without which all other knowledge is not only meaningless but dangerous. The True Church calls to the service of religion the gifts of science, art and philosophy and hallows them. It calls to its ministry the love-inspired and compassionate efforts of educational, social and healing agencies, most of which are children of the Church who have forgotten their parentage. It hallows their efforts and gives them a spiritual incentive.

These are the qualities of the True Church, now struggling for life in a generation sick almost beyond its redeeming and saving power.

III

When did it begin?

It is always interesting to contemplate those first beginnings. We see the development of a great system, a great plan. We impute a purpose, a Planner, one who saw from the beginning clear through to the end, one who not only willed the achievement of human personality but the possibility of fellowship.

We see primitive men huddled together in a cave, driven there by cold and danger of wild beasts. In their nearness human kinship was born, and out of it came fellowship and love. When some early tribe dwelt for a time by a river where the land was fertile, love of land and country began.

Perhaps one night as he sat on a rock watching the moon come up, one of these primitive men sighted along a boulder and marked it with an oyster shell to indicate the place. Night after night he waited, watching the same process, until he discovered that twenty-nine days later the moon came up at the identical place. Thus might have been born a recognition of one fact of the predictability of our natural world. In like manner, perhaps, some individual later discovered a law that governed human relationships—the knowledge that, if two or more people acted in a certain way, all of them gained greater good than if they acted singly. Out of such accumulated insights came the thrilling formulation of the Ten Commandments, and from them sprang, ultimately, the law of love.

Forty-three centuries B.C., the Egyptians made their first-hand observations of the movements of the heavenly bodies, keeping accurate records of these observations and drawing from them the sound conclusions of a calendar of 365 days. These early Egyptians observed human behavior also, for by 4000 B.C. they had developed a legal system that governed human relations.

In 3200 B.C. Menes became the first human lawgiver in Egyptian tradition. In 2900 B.C. an Egyptian king made the first recorded expedition overseas, broadening the knowledge and vision of the Egyptians. About 2500 B.C. the Chinese legal system came into being, the most ancient in human history that has survived until now. A few years ago a fragment of one of the Sumerian legal codes was discovered and deciphered, dating from 2400 B.C. Man's long struggle to establish a way of life for the common good continued, and in 2050 B.C. the Hammurabi code was developed.

It is noteworthy that apparently man first began to study the stars and the predictability of the world, then the laws that governed his relations with others, and last the source of the plans and the knowledge of the Planner, which did not come until fifteen hundred years before Christ. Hinduism, the oldest living organized religion in the world, though in part a social caste system, does have within it a concept of the Divine, His purpose, and plan. In 1375 B.C., 2866 years after the introduction of the Egyptian calendar based on science, the Egyptian king, Akhenaten, introduced the worship of one God. He promulgated the ideas of universal love of God and universal brotherhood of man. He, therefore, became the first great trail blazer before Christ.

The Jews were the first racial group to hold persistently to the idea of one God. Moses, the Egyptian born and reared Jew, who led his fellow Jews out of Egyptian bondage in 1200 B.C., formulated the Decalogue, the result of thousands of years of seeking and striving. The Ten Commandments are, to this day, basic to all our legal practice. Moses was another of the trail blazers.

About 600 B.C. came a new plan—a legal system that is not conceived as a part of religion emanating from a divine source. It was the first move toward a plan for providing justice through court trial. About 500 B.C. came Confucius, one of the world's wisest men and chief justice in China. His philosophy covers the whole range of personal morality and practical politics and has now pervaded Chinese life for twenty-four hundred years. He first formulated the "golden rule" in history, stated negatively: "Do not do unto others what you would not want them to do to you." He was the second person to bring the vision of brotherhood. He said, "Within the four seas all are older brothers and younger brothers."

No one, however, has better charted the trail forward to the birth of Christ than the Old Testament prophets. They foretold the nature of his birth, the nature of his mission, even Calvary. Isaiah speaks of him, "And his name shall be called wonderful, Counsellor, the Mighty God, the Everlasting Father, the Prince of Peace . . . the Lord hath laid on him the iniquities of us all."

It was within the Jewish tradition especially that the hope of a Messiah grew. Finally, with Jesus' birth, the wisdom of all the ages became manifest in one body, in one soul, in one mind. He came to live completely by the attitudes of God, so that the mind of God became the mind in Jesus for all humanity.

Jesus would never have appeared if there had not been others who blazed the trail and if millions of people had not looked for his coming. In Jesus there was the culmination of ages of longing, of striving, of seeking, and the Divine response. Out of his three years of teaching and living with his disciples, came our knowledge of the way and the truth and the life. After his resurrection, the Church reached the truest form it has ever achieved in history.

It was then that the early Church battled the world and became a mighty redeeming force. Paul referred to its spiritual power in these words, "It is the Church of the living God, the pillar and ground of truth." In his age Paul saw the moral verities assaulted on every side. Today, too, they are attacked by the subtle sophistries of men's minds, by the undisciplined passions of their bodies. Selfishness, greed and indulgence threaten to overflow and engulf the individual of today; but still, amid the war and welter of the ages, God's ideal for men is imperial command to each loyal soul. Through them the truth continues to live. Although often obscured and hidden, this truth has ever been alive from the beginning. Here and there throughout history, it is glimpsed, discovered, and becomes incarnate, even while the ways of enmity and falsehood beat fiercely against it. But age after age, when the storm has passed, the truth throws the undivided splendor of its light across the waters of time. Then the ideals of the True Church show forth, like a tower emerging from rifting clouds. As the spirit of Paul's teachings makes clear, the strategy of God in His Church; the strength of moral truth is in a body of men and women united in a consecrated comradeship—worshiping at the shrine of Life, walking in its radiance and exulting in its word and action. In another challenging insight to this union of people who are followers of Christ, the apostle says, "For through him we both have access by one Spirit unto the Father. Now, therefore ye are no more strangers and foreigners, but fellowcitizens with the saints, and of the household of God; and are built upon the foundation of the apostles and prophets, Jesus Christ himself being the chief corner stone; in whom all the building fitly framed together groweth unto an holy temple in the Lord: In whom ye also are builded together for an habitation of God through the Spirit."

Through the years, in relative degrees, the Church has kept alive a heart of compassion. At its best it has provided an enlightened conscience and has been the custodian of glorious gospel. Always there has been a remnant, a few like those who belonged to the company of Anna of whom it was said that she waited for the redemption of Israel. The followers of Jesus in the earlier Church had a power that the later Church lost and has never fully recovered since Augustine, even in the most spiritually vivid years of its history. But always there has been a remnant—those few who waited for the morning, who wished for the dawn, who came from high places and low, who kept the flame of their faith burning on the altars of their hearts. Amid the spiritual sterility and lethargy of their times they were divinely discontent, wistful, devout, expectant. They were the pious puritans of England, the persecuted Presbyterians of the Scotch Highlands, the Waldenseans of the Italian mountains, the members of the Dutch church during the last war, who would be drawn together secretly in barns or cottage kitchens or woodland glens to spend some hours in prayer and study of the Word. In all ages they have lived—those who scanned the stormy horizon watching for the dawn—those who in the darkest night confidently expected the daybreak. What a debt civilization owes them!

IV

What is its purpose?

The purpose of the True Church is to help each individual to become alive with God in his soul. Its place in the plan of the Divine is to help persons fulfill the purpose of creation. Only as individuals are right within, will human relations be right. Two insights are common to all religions: we are spiritual, and the purpose of life is to develop our spiritual natures. To study Aldous Huxley's *Perennial Philosophy*, is to see in consecrated souls of all ages a validation of these facts. Jesus said, "Seek ye first the kingdom of God ... and all these things shall be added unto you." It is the mission of the True Church so to guide growing life that the Kingdom of God may come into individual and collective living.

It should be stated at the very start, and most emphatically, that there is no contradiction or disharmony between individual and collective religious living. A conflict, indeed, is often precipitated between them; an antithesis is drawn between saving one's own soul and devotion to the social order. This conflict is utterly unreal. The solitary monk, the idealist in his ivory tower, on the one hand, and the secular-minded reformer on the other, are equally one-sided, and in the end each defeats the purposes he professes to cherish. Man is a dual creature. Neither his spiritual nor his physical component can deny the presence of the other. The True Church is neither divine nor human exclusively: the True Church is both at once, indissolubly. This false line between the eternal and the temporal, it is the function of the Church to abolish. The church building contains both an altar and a parish hall. And throughout the pages that follow, when I concentrate my attention on one, I do not imply that the other has ceased to exist.

We are all interested in building a better world. Yet, as we study the New Testament and the writings of saints of all ages, we reach the conclusion that Jesus' fundamental teaching of the Kingdom had to do with men's souls and not with their social institutions. In our modern Western thought, we have grown very impatient with that spiritual culture which Jesus stressed. What we want is a kinder, more just social order, a more equitable distribution of the income from wealth, more leisure, better living and working conditions. If we have these, we reason, we shall find their by-products in finer spiritual culture and higher moral tone. But with all the words that are spoken and written in support of this oversanguine thesis, only an occasional modern prophet points with an admonitory finger to the crux of our situation. Bruce Hutchinson of the Winnepeg *Free Press*, writing from Washington, had this to say:

The paramount question is not whether the American people can solve the political and economic problems of the world but whether they can solve the problems of their own life, the problem of maintaining the old integrity of that life against the disease of luxury which invariably sapped all groups of men who enjoyed luxury in the long past.

Against all advocates of social salvation by quick and easy methods, we can point to the necessities of the individual's inner life. Here is a thought that focuses on the real interest of Christ and the other God-centered individuals of history. To Jesus, the Kingdom began with the reign of God in the individual soul. It is the consciousness of God, enthusiastic, regnant, bringing every thought and desire into captivity until the heart is aflame with love for Him and all that He loves. The Kingdom of God is an experience of Him that controls the motives of the soul. The life Jesus lived here among men is the Kingdom of God. Jesus is himself the best illustration of his teaching.

Jesus believed that the primary need of men was a rediscovery of God—not a redefinition, but a rediscovery; not an intellectual concept, but a spiritual apprehension. All the evil of men's lives, all the maladjustment of our social system, Jesus would charge to diseased souls. He would change institutions by changing men. To our pragmatic Western way of thinking, these are alien ideas. We place our faith in organizations, in reforms, in legislation. Given the chance to use our organizational technique, we believe that we can create our own kingdom wherein righteousness shall dwell, and that a reformed society will make better men. Our faith in social and economic reform is naïve, almost youthfully ingenuous. Rebellious against the necessity of changing our own hearts, impatient of the slow processes of spiritual culture, and unwilling to give ourselves to such a task, we have undertaken to build a superstructure without laying a proper foundation.

Thus Jesus was a disappointment to the social reformers of his day, as he is to the same group in our own. He did not attack where they thought he ought to attack. He lived under a ruthless political tyranny at a time when a few huge fortunes rose like islands in a surrounding sea of poverty. It was a time when the poor lived perilously near to starvation and the rich were satiated with luxury. At such a time, what did Jesus do? He stood on a grassy hill in Galilee and said: "Blessed are the poor in spirit: for theirs is the kingdom of heaven . . . Blessed are the meek: for they shall inherit the earth . . . Blessed are the pure in heart: for they shall see God." No one of these utterances has to do with the social conditions of his time, but with the souls of men. Either Jesus, as many affirm, had no understanding of the terrible sins of social life, or he had another way of attacking these evils. He did speak of the perils of wealth, but his chief concern seemed to be the danger of its misuses in dwarfing the soul. Jesus did not believe one could make a just society of unjust men; he could see no hope of a kingdom of kindness made up of men whose hearts were hardened in hate. But Jesus undertook to cleanse the stream at its secret source. His way was to persuade men to surrender to God in the inmost sanctuaries of their souls. He knew that individual and social religion are mutually dependent.

A social salvation, a kindly kingdom of brotherhood, yes—but a kingdom founded on hearts cleansed and motivated by divine love. That is the program of Jesus. When the Pharisees came to him and asked "when the kingdom of God should come," the answer of Jesus was, "The kingdom of God cometh not with observation: Neither shall men say, Lo here! or, lo there! for, behold, the kingdom of God is within you." The Kingdom is not a new theory of God, it is a new experience of God. It is not merely a new sociology, but a new experience of the transforming power of God's love. The Kingdom of God is the complete sovereignty of God in the souls of men. And it is inevitable that such a sovereignty will reflect itself in a society organized to do the will of God.

But let us go a little further in our search for meanings. What is the nature of this inner Kingdom? What differences does it make in life? What are the spiritual values by which it may be known?

Jesus often used two words which will help us answer these questions: faith and fear. The experience of God in the soul is the enthronement of faith and the banishment of fear. When Jesus spoke of faith he was not thinking about codes or creeds. He was not thinking about intellectual opinion. He was talking about an inner attitude toward life. He spoke of the soul's approach to life and God. To Jesus, faith was a calm fundamental expectancy of good based on the conviction that at the center of the universe is a fatherly heart. To him, faith was a mighty creative power and all things were possible to them that believed.

We have well nigh lost this rich meaning of faith in our obsession with externals, and certainly we have too largely lost the secret of its power. In our personal lives, we are in bondage to fear. Overborn with anxiety, we grow old before our time. We are afraid of life and afraid of death; we fear illness and failure and old age. Even sin is a subtle form of fear. Fear paralyzes, faith releases; fear torments, faith inspires; fear narrows the vision, faith enlarges the horizon; fear blinds, faith clarifies; fear inhibits the moral initiatives, faith taps the deepest springs of life.

Persistent pessimism, sullen cynicism, contempt, these are the brood of fear. Often they parade a superior sophistication. But deadening disillusion is no better for having a university diploma. A great age is most often the product of a great faith. Under the sunlight of divine confidence, listening souls have caught the song of angels and have translated it into the enduring music of the world. Out of the visions of believing hearts, hearts that heard other footfalls on the hills, have come immortal loveliness in picture and poem. There is in life but one fundamental falsehood, one dark and dire heresy. It is this: to believe that life is not so good a thing as we had thought; that our dreams and hopes are nobler than the possible reality. It was against this heresy of the heart that Jesus spoke these simple, sublime, words: "In my father's house are many mansions: if it were not so, I would have told you. . . . Think your best, live for the highest, dream divinely—if your hopes went beyond reality, I, who love truth and know life would have told you."

In spite of that assurance, fears of the heart have projected themselves into our collective life. We ignore the fact that the whole progress of society has been the slow and painful conquest of fear by faith. It is faith alone that has made it possible for men to live together. Families began to believe a little, one in the other, and out of that first furtive faith came the social unit called the tribe. After weary years of turmoil, the tribe at the foot of this mountain began to trust the one over the river, and they, too, began to believe a little in the third one whose village was by the woodland lake. Out of that belief the small nation was created, then the larger nation. Every step in the willing association of people has been a step of faith. But fear is still dominant in associated life. Each nation imputes to other nations motives more ignoble than its own. And so distrust begets distrust; suspicion breeds suspicion. In this atmosphere are born the intrigues, the secret diplomacy, the lies and deception out of which issues the ageless wickedness of war.

We are living in a rapidly shrinking world. We cannot always be huddled together in shuddering terror. We must learn our common interests, our common aspirations, our common humanity. By faith we are saved; not by force of arms, not by fear that outruns fear, but by faith—faith in God's high purposes and faith in man. This is Jesus' message and the vision of the saints of all ages. Through generation after generation, they have been calling, "Thy kingdom come!" Let the glowing morn of faith scatter the dark gloom of fear.

Modern life has been entirely changed by the invention and utilization of machinery. Next to the birth of Jesus, nothing, with the possible exception of the discovery of printing, has so influenced the life of the world as the mass employment of machines. In Kennedy's analogy of contemporary life, two great arms of steel reach out, slowly and surely binding into one bundle the life of the world. This is being achieved by two mighty conquests,—the conquest of time and the conquest of space. Rapid transportation and lightninglike communication are erasing distance. At the same time, the laborer's tools have been taken from his hands. In their place have developed great factories which the laborer cannot guide and control but for whose use he depends upon someone else.

All life becomes more and more interdependent. Nationalism, too—the fierce and selfish nationalism of our world today—is a protective reaction on the part of peoples who find themselves suddenly brushing elbows with their world neighbors. In a few fleeting years, the machine has thrown together into one heap diverse races, creeds, and nations. Upon the peoples of the world has been thrust the sheer necessity of learning to live together, to work together, to co-operate in a human enterprise. To many the arms of steel seem now, as Mr. Kennedy says, "like the tentacles of an octopus relentlessly crushing mankind into a herd of stampeding, fighting animals, destroying life and beauty and bathing the world in blood." Yet those same arms of steel which seem now to destroy may well be transformed into the shadow of God's wings as He gathers His children together in one high, human understanding.

Only as the Church, empowered by the Holy Spirit, helps individuals achieve union with God in themselves and with others, is it the True Church. To achieve this end, the True Church works directly to guide the growth of the individual and the development of community relations that will keep persons free.

V

How is its purpose fulfilled in individual lives?

Thousands of members of the contemporary Church truly wish to seek first the Kingdom. They are eager. Thousands come into the Church seeking to know union with God, desiring to discover the purpose of life and the will of God. But only a few succeed in growing above the vegetative level. Many of them withdraw from the Church, to live individually and in small groups more truly akin to the True Church of the living God than is the contemporary Church itself.

In these years of crises, many members of the contemporary Church find themselves in the plight of the singer of the 73rd Psalm, but few achieve the growth of the divine in their souls as did he. It is important that we see illustrated the process of spiritual growth.

"As for me, my feet were almost gone; my steps had well nigh slipped . . ." begins the 73rd Psalm. And it ends, "God is the strength of my heart, and my portion forever." Between them is the deep experience of a soul's growth, the descent of a human spirit from sunlit heights of faith to dark caverns of despair, and its struggle back again to dawnlit hills of hope.

This is a man who had lived by great beliefs until, in his hour of crisis, he almost threw them aside forever in exchange for the hand-to-mouth philosophy of the world. After discouragement, the deepening darkness of doubt, and the despairing search for refuge, a hand clasped his in the moonlight and the darkness began to fade before the light of dawn-drenched hills. Then a little song burst forth in the hidden places of his heart, and the song became a shout of victory in the market place. Such was the experience of this poet of long ago.

His faith, strong in youth, wavered. Grown to a man, he looked out upon the world and saw it as it was. The romance of his youthful religion gave way to the harsh facts of life. "Behold, these are the ungodly, who prosper in the world," he wrote. "They are not in trouble as other men . . . They are corrupt, and speak wickedly concerning oppression: they speak loftily. They set their mouth against the heavens, and their tongue walketh through the earth." And our poet cries, "Verily I have cleansed my heart in vain, and washed my hands in innocency."

His is a problem as old as life and as new as this day's dawn. And it is no academic query of a doctrinaire speculating on the evil of the world; it is a tragic moment. His whole life depends upon the decision of the hour. Either there is moral law running through all of life and history, or there is not. Either the universe is on the side of goodness, or it is not. Is there nothing but a vast indifference? He must know. He cannot fight on the side of an illusion. Amid the mockery of unbelief and the harsh cruelties of iniquitous living, let God rise up and make Himself known. Here is an epic discouragement. It is not petty impatience with the failure of personal plans, nor whining because some little ship of human desire failed to make the harbor. Here is no childish threat: "Life, coddle me, cushion my way or I shall not believe in God!" Here is a great reflective soul looking realistically at the world and finding for the moment no basis for faith. He mourns neither the loss of fortune nor the loss of family but the fact that he can find no footsteps of God on the highway of history. He listens, and amid the raucous clamor of selfishness and sin, he can hear no whisper of the voice of God. And is this not where the contemporary Church falls short? This, indeed, is where the True Church meets its most triumphant test.

It is plain that both the impotence of our generation and the weakness and secularization of our religion are born of an easy, vague and undemanding theology. God has been an affiliate. He is a member emeritus of society. We have made of Him a God who gives celestial sanction to our own prejudices and desires. The Holy One, in whose hands the nations are as a drop of water in the sea, we have forgotten. We have instead a hazy, humanized God whose activity is seen vaguely everywhere and clearly nowhere. We have lost the God for whose glory we exist. We have lost the only reason for life in our failure to do His will. Macaulay said of the Puritans, "They feared nothing but God." Of our generation some historian may yet write: They feared everything but God.

Millions of people, especially in recent years, feel exactly as did the psalmist. They cannot help but think that it is the wicked and arrogant and God-defying who prosper. "Pride compasseth them about as a chain; violence covereth them as a garment." There has never been a moment in history when the surface look of the human scene would lead men to believe that theirs is a morally governed universe. There has never been a time when the workings of a righteous God were so evident that men were constrained to believe in Him. Always on the surface scene of history is the triumph of the iniquitous and the godless. It is easy to look back, to isolate a phase of any civilization and think: "Ah, to have been alive in such a time would have been ecstasy indeed."

But that is romance. Any man with a passion for justice in his soul would have walked the streets of ancient Athens with a broken heart. The Augustan Era of Rome produced, at best, only a few flowers in the slimy swamps of falsehood and tyranny. There certainly was nothing in the human scene of Jesus' day to make men believe in a sovereign God. Religion was a rigid set of rights and rules, the temple a place of commerce and human exploitation, the priesthood corrupt and worldly. Likewise these past few decades when most of us were lulled to sleep by the theory of inevitable progress have not been a time when men turned to God. Indeed, this has been a time when secularism reached its zenith. All of the prosperity we now know is but a pallid blush on the cheek of a consumptive society.

We do not find God easily. Men have never found, nor will ever find, Him fully by inductive means—by searching the events of contemporary history, by picking up a bit of evidence here, something of proof there; by observing injustice punished yonder, righteousness rewarded here, and at last concluding: Surely God is here. I have found Him. God is good to Israel, to such as are of pure heart. The first look at the human scene is always discouraging to the seeker after God. Wickedness is always obvious and obtrusive and clamorous, seeming to dominate the state. But we must face the facts. We are not living in a world of exact moral requital. We ought to be glad this is not a world where evil is immediately punished in kind and where virtue receives quick and obvious reward. Such a world would be without grace, without generosity and magnanimity. Where would we be if a law of exact requital prevailed, if life had never been better to us than we deserved?

The evidences of God in history are certain but rarely obvious. They do not float upon the surface of the stream. God is neither earthquake nor whirlwind. He is the still, small voice often unheeded by the passing throng. When the poet of the 73rd Psalm sang his dirge of discouragement, where was God? He was in the poet's own soul as he knelt in the temple, crying, "Woe is me, I am unclean."

In those days following the crucifixion of Christ, who could have realized that God was not with the Roman legions marching along the roads of the great empire, but with a Jew named Paul, preaching from ghetto to ghetto in the Greco-Roman world? If we had been looking for God in proud, voluptuous, decaying Athens three centuries earlier, would we readily have found Him? But He was there, in the heart of a good and humble man, Socrates, whose prayer was: "Give me beauty in the outward soul. May the outward and inward be one. May I reckon the wise to be wealthy and may I have such a quantity of gold as a temperate man and he only can carry."

Finally the writer of the psalm tells us how his triumph was achieved. Did he suddenly see some dramatic victory of right over wrong? Did he behold the wicked cry out in sackcloth and ashes? Not at all. He says, "Until I went into the sanctuary of God; then understood I their end." And he gives lyric expression to his experience of God. "Thou shalt guide me with thy counsel, and afterward receive me to glory. Whom have I in heaven but thee? and there is none upon earth that I desire beside thee."

How rarely does the contemporary Church lead the in-

dividual to the true sanctuary! The True Church begins where
the stumbling feet of the searcher first hesitate. It leads them,
encourages them, guides them to the heart of the sanctuary
itself. The certainty of God's government is found not by observation but by communion. It comes not by science but by
surrender. It lies not in the knowledge of the laboratory but in
the secret of the sanctuary. Those who have been very sure of
God have pillared their certainty upon their own soul's fellowship with Him. This is the lesson of Job. This is the testimony
of the prophets. Know God by your own dedication to His
Holy Will. Live in communion with Him and you will see
Him in the rise and fall of the tides of history. It was not history that made Jesus sure of God. He said, "These have not
known Thee, but I have known Thee."

The seeking mind may justifiably ask: were not the prophets
always interpreting history as the reward or punishment of
God? Of course they were. But they did not find God exclusively
in history. They found Him primarily in their souls and
brought their vision to the interpretation of history. Amos found
God under the stars in the wilderness; Isaiah in the hour of
despair in the temple; Jeremiah in the quiet of little orchard-
girt Anathoth. That is the secret of the spiritual life. In giving
the reasons why they cannot believe in God, many today conclude: The climax of it all is war; there cannot be a God if
such a horror is permitted. To them Isaiah and Jeremiah would
say, "The nations have lived for years as though there were no
God. See the awful catastrophe that has ensued, see what proof
history gives of the God of righteousness we know in our own
souls." While some observers see man as a victim, the prophets
see him as a violator of the will of God. Only in the prophetic
view is there hope. For if nature, or fate, or some cruel absolute

causes war, there will never be any chance for peace. One cannot reform the absolute. But if man's sins make war, if God is on the side of peace and justice; if the violation of His will results in such awful calamity, then there is hope. Then man can surrender to God's sovereign will and know the dawn of hope and peace.

The Church must begin to ask: Do you want to find God in these disturbing times? Do you want steady feet on these unsteady ways? God is bound to act. He is bound to pour Himself into you as soon as He finds you ready. Finding us ready, He is bound to overflow us, just as the sun bursts forth when the air is bright and clear. He is no farther off than the door of our hearts. He stands lingering, waiting for whoever is ready to open the door and let Him in. We need not call from afar.

But it is not as easy as these words may indicate. We are chained to the earth. We are enclosed in a physical cycle. We move in groups, and we are related in social life with others who live in the body and rarely rise above the carnal level. We need the True Church, to help us on every day of every week, from birth to the end of earthly existence. We need the True Church to find God in prayer, in deep surrender, and to help us live with God in the fellowship of His love. In so living, men shall know that God has not abdicated. They shall have serene confidence. Arrogant wickedness will have its little day and die. But abiding still when the last star has faded and the last sun has sunk to rest, abiding forever are men's faith and hope and love, and the greatest of all is love. Knowing God in the sanctuary of the soul, they shall not lose Him in the tragedies of life or in the cataclysms of history.

"I went into the sanctuary and then I understood." It was not a verbal revelation that the psalmist received. He was lifted to a new level of thought and feeling. God lifted him above the bitter hour through which he was passing, and he found security. "Nevertheless I am with thee!" Despairing, he entered; confident, he came out. He did not find a complete explanation of life. He found God; that was enough.

Such is the quality of those who make the True Church. The True Church enfolds children at birth, teaching them divine truth, keeping them free to grow in the way by which the life that is God may become life eternal in them. Only as the Church teaches youth does it fulfill its true mission in the world. The fact that our children have a date with the future is clearly recognized by every dictator, by every opportuning demagogue and political doctrinaire. What a dire catastrophe comes to pass when the contemporary Church forgets it!

The True Church represents the moral hope of society. Clearly the lines are being drawn. Clearly the struggle is between the Church of the living God and the revived paganism of the pre-Christian era. Leadership in this moral struggle must and will come only from a True Church in which individuals come alive with the very life of God.

II

IT IS THE GROWING FELLOWSHIP
OF THE WAY

THE True Church is the fellowship of the way to divine life in the soul of the individual and in the collective life of the community. All man's activity is inalienably religious. We have seen the failure of the contemporary Church to lead individuals into the way. We have seen how it has compromised with the truth by which the life that is God becomes life eternal in the soul. We have seen how, in spite of the Church, the love that is God has become a poor makeweight in the balance of human relationships rather than the ruling spirit of the universe. This failure, we implied, is due to the confusion regarding the mission of the Church, to its effort to help people live both in harmony with the sensate world and in loyalty to the life of the spirit, and to the divided and competitive fellowship of the Church.

The Church's mission is to keep people free or, if freedom has not been achieved, to help them become free for the fullest achievement of the Kingdom of God within the soul. We have sought to make clear the nature of this Kingdom and we have endeavored to illustrate the process of achievement in the life of an ancient searcher who sought and reached the goal.

John G. McKenzie says:

Our social order is the creation of individuals; it is sustained by the energy and aims of individuals. The modern world, with its dictators and totalitarian forms of government, illustrates the dictum of Carlyle that the history of a nation is just the biographies of its leading individuals. It is true that once a social order is created it has an objective existence and begins to shape the individual. We must be careful, however, to realize what that means. It does not mean that the social order is a living thing that exerts an irresistible power upon individuals. No! *We are shaped by the social order in the sense that we have to fit ourselves into it.* When a social order is changed it is because some individual challenged its assumptions, refused to fit into; and thus a movement for change was instituted.

That is why the Gospel seems to have so little to say to society as such. Christ deals with that which produces social order, that which creates or changes a social order—the individual. Society is the product of personality, and personality is always individual; there is no such thing as a group personality.[1]

The True Church implies the sort of society free individuals naturally and inevitably create.

Dr. Egbert Munzer, of St. Xavier University in Nova Scotia, makes this pertinent comment:

The future will not belong to the organizers or the politicians of the traditional type, but to the saints and the prophets, and thus to the religionists, and it will be *they* who become the creators, neither capitalism nor socialism which after all are fundamentally the same, inverted and twisted but intrinsically related *querelles domestiques.*

The influence of the True Church is set in time, though it reaches beyond time. It begins before the individual is conceived, making sure that the parents who co-operate with God in bringing new life into the world have found union with God within themselves and with each other, and that they are one in com-

[1] *Pastoral Psychology and Psychotherapy*, by John G. McKenzie (New York: The Macmillan Company, 1941), p. 16.

plete surrender to His will. The True Church seeks for each child not only that he be conceived and born in love but also that he be kept free for the fulfillment of the purpose of creation. Throughout the individual's life span, it continues its guidance. Finally, when earthly life is ended, the True Church again reaches beyond time and beyond death, pointing the way to immortality.

The True Church begets the home as the most important relationship for the child's true growth. Men are no more solitary religiously than in their human activities. The True Church seeks to help build a house into a home, a hearth into an altar, and the family into a unit of the Kingdom of God. With this as its primary training ground, the Church is interested in promoting growth in all the areas of life: in the relations of friendship, to give support to the spiritual quest; in the business of working and earning, to augment the security of all men and to advance brotherhood in the common search for bread, always putting soul above body; in the enjoyment of play and leisure, to recreate the soul and renew the body; in the sacrament of marriage, to foster its development as a permanent, spiritual, lifetime union between husband, wife and God. The True Church is interested in all aspects of the collective will of government and non-government, locally, nationally and universally, seeking passionately to make the will of God the will of men. It is interested in promoting growth in prayer and worship, placing major emphasis first on the will of God, on the life that is God, on the love of God, on the full expression of God in all the relations of life; and, second, on a virile fellowship between the individual and the universal community.

The True Church uses a place of meeting as a training center for teaching the spiritual life, as a concentration point where reciprocal ministries are stimulated for the fullest Christian sharing and sustaining; as an area where all the resources of living may be mobilized for co-operation with the divine in building God's Kingdom; and especially as a sanctuary for corporate and private worship that issues in growth in all aspects of sacramental living. In the building it uses, the True Church is as interested in the nursery as it is in the sermons preached from its pulpit; it spends as much money on leading youth as it does on comforting age. It looks upon the Sunday services as only one aspect of religious expression. Its building is open seven days and nights and its ministry covers all seasons.

I

Here is a boy, Gene, for example, conceived and born in love. He came to think of God, the Giver, the loving Heavenly Father, as naturally as he came into all other aspects of knowledge. From the beginning he learned to appreciate what money can never buy—beauty, the natural world, the love of others, the thrill of creating from materials and in imagination. Out of his sense of belonging grew a wholesome independence. He learned to identify certain activities as the God-way, others as the destructive way. It was God's way to co-operate, to share, to be honest, to help others, to seek the will of God in all things. When he encountered bafflement or disagreement, he was taught to join with others of his family in seeking the will of God. There were times when he refused to accept that will. There were times of stubbornness and rebellion. But gradually he came to follow the God-way, not because he thought he should, but because to him it was more real and more natural than the destructive way. His parents prayed with and for him. The family spent a period each evening in prayer and Bible study and, as Gene and his sister grew older, each member of the family learned the joy and power of worship and prayer.

From Gene's infancy, the Church was as familiar as his home. To go to the church building and to share in activities that centered there was natural. He loved it as his parents did. It was a strong, continuing love. While in college, he hitchhiked many miles to worship in his home church. From babyhood on, the teachings within the church building had confirmed what his home had taught, and had given him training in all phases of religious expression and leadership.

At the age of fourteen Gene was baptized, and became a part of the Church. This involved no radical change, simply a stage in his growth. He entered a vital youth fellowship. Gene and his sister were in the heart of it. Here again he found the same quality of fellowship as in his home. Here he was ever supported in his search for the best and was challenged to give his best to the fellowship. His life centered in his home and in his church.

In high school he failed to make the Hi-Y Club or a fraternity, because he did not go in for the particular stereotypes which the ruling group considered the marks of a real fellow. These did not fit his pattern. It made little difference, however, for his life was filled by his church and his home. When he went to college, he joined a fraternity which never became important beyond giving him his first experience with a fellowship that supported living on the level of modern secularisms. His college work did focus his vocational interests, gave him confidence, and set him to the purpose of becoming a medical missionary.

As Gene grew up, he came into an understanding of himself, of the urges of life, of the methods others use to satisfy them. It was a simple, natural achievement of understanding. Gene had become a person, loving God and devoted to the God-way, and at the same time loving the fellowship of those who shared that way. His home and his church were always his first love. Out of the inner serenity which they gave him, he was able to share with others who differed from him in spiritual ideals.

Looking back over his youth, Gene finds that the Church confirmed all his home had taught, and added information, training and a supporting fellowship in the search of God's will. In addition, it taught him the love of great music, a respect where his home had failed. His college life confirmed all these teachings and helped him to focus his intellectual and social interests on the work of medical missions. His religion was a mode and pattern of actual behavior.

On a summer evening in Canada, Gene discussed with his father the qualities he desired in a wife. At the close of the evening, father and son both made a compact to pray that God would guide him to such a woman. In the following fall, a girl of missionary parents in China came to Gene's community and attended the same church college group with him. Remarkably akin in spiritual development, they found friendship, then love. Both put first the will of God. Both loved the Church, finding in it their deepest fellowship outside of the home. Together they shared the beauty of worship, the wonder of the out-of-doors, the life-giving secret of music, the lure of truth and of life itself. It was for both their first love. Their marriage was and is a sacrament born of God.

What has been wrought in the lives of Gene and his young wife is the primary purpose of the Church. By simple, natural means youth must be kept free from all that blocks, delays or hinders the growth of the spirit. The challenge is primarily to the home and to those experiences that center in the program of the Church itself. Since the best way to guide a boy effectively is to guide the crowd he runs with, the True Church is concerned about the life, instruction and influence of the school and the playground. Although the True Church does not seek to control the school, its leaders work very closely with school leaders. Only those teachers and administrators who carry in their souls an understanding of the spiritual purpose of life can help the learner discover the eternal truth without which all other knowledge either has no significance or may be fraught with peril.

How shall the Church keep the individual free to seek first the Kindom of God, the rule of God's will in the soul? There are some specific emphases the True Church makes throughout the years of growth. It aims at introducing each child to life in a family unit which is alert to the will of God. It tries to insure that the child is well loved and that he learns to love in return, growing in time to that high level where his own love of God flows through him and out to others, irrespective of color, creed or station in life.[2]

The True Church recognizes and attempts to provide for certain basic needs of youth, and to channel its energies in appropriate habits. Youth needs to belong to a group where fellowship is at its best and where, at the same time, individual self can find true expression. It needs the assurance of self-earned recognition in order to live with security among others. It needs to live with others who seek first to know and love God. And greatest of all is youth's need to know God as the primary source of all values, rather than to hold to the values as an end in themselves.

[2] This thought is graphically presented in *Bringing up Ourselves*, by Helen Gibson Hogue (New York: Charles Scribner's Sons, 1943).

For each child the True Church seeks a home where his body is given the best of care and where his soul is nurtured with prayer and skill and sensitivity. The body is the child's earthly house; it should be kept clean, it should grow strong, it should develop all of its potentialities for the fullest service. But the body's true reality is the soul. It is the purpose of the True Church to quicken that soul with the understanding of God, to integrate powers that otherwise suffer dissipation.

Later in this chapter we shall discuss the ministry of freeing those blocked from God's grace. Let it be said here that the nature of the home into which a child is born is of the utmost significance. The ideal is for those who marry always to have been free themselves; that together they have as their primary interest the finding of union with God and the fulfillment of the purpose of their creation. If two persons are akin in this respect, their choice of each other is wise. The True Church helps people understand that, when choice is based chiefly on personal attractiveness or has a sensual emphasis, the marriage is always precariously founded. In such marriages the chances are small indeed that children will grow naturally in the life of the spirit, no matter how closely they are related to the Church. Each time the Church keeps two persons free for the fullest spiritual growth in marriage, its most important contribution to the unborn child has been made.

The True Church does all in its power to help every one of its children grow into maturity dedicated to the purpose of our creation. Within its ministry there is always a twofold emphasis: the parents, and the children. The home is the Church embodied and in action. Central in its ministry is the training of parents to be the child's first teacher of religion, his first interpreter of the spiritual life. The Church has classes for expectant parents.

In these groups are discussions with regard to the spiritual relationship of parents, their prayer life, their commitment to the will of God, their freedom from bondage to things that are incompatible with God's Kingdom. New parents are given constant guidance for those early days during which the child can develop either a loving or a hostile attitude toward life, become secure or insecure, overdependent or wholesomely independent.

The True Church provides reciprocal guidance for young and older parents during all stages of child growth. A program such as this is wide in scope, potentially far-reaching in its effects. It is therefore important to discuss in some detail specific guidance techniques and other means by which the program can be implemented.

By means of a group-counseling process, parents of younger children may share their problems with one another and with those who have been especially successful in meeting similar difficulties. The emphasis should always be on guiding the child positively rather than on waiting until a real problem arises. Demonstrations are helpful. A day nursery is invaluable in the program, giving the very young child his first group experience in the church. Parents should be invited to observe in the nursery methods of living with children. Implications of what they see should be discussed later. An overcoercive parent may receive far more help by observation than through discussion.

For those parents who are baffled, there are clinics or group interviews. These are far more to the point than personal conferences, as a rule, for when problems are shared, the objectivity of those concerned is increased. To know that someone else has the same problem is a help. The sharing of parental experience assists all and creates a bond of understanding.

When children are consecrated or baptized, the parents are

led through a special period of study so that they may grow in understanding the meaning of their vows. Before the first experience of school, the parents are given a chance to discuss with other parents the best way to prepare the child for his initial venture into school life. When the child comes to puberty, parents receive help in giving a spiritual interpretation and a wholesome physical background for the sexual urge, and for friendship and love. They are helped to understand the physical, mental and spiritual changes which come with the dawning of manhood and womanhood.

The use of a personality inventory such as the one by Lois Leon Thurston or Robert G. Bernreuter helps the early adolescent understand the nature of his approach to life; whether he is objective or given to mood swings, whether dependent or independent, extroverted or introverted, dominant or submissive, self-confident or self-conscious, sociable or unsociable. One local church has followed this practice for ten years. The results have been encouraging. Out of 637 persons from that church who went into the armed services during the war, not one failed emotionally.

Before these inventories are given out, the parents are invited to a series of conferences. One church finds that the parents frequently ask to use them too. When the chart of a boy or girl comes home, the parent is prepared not only to help the child understand the results of his inventory, but also to help him in his new program of personal growth. Parents need the opportunity to share in all the interests of adolescence: friendships and the choice of a life mate. They meet regularly and plan ways to help their young people live as Christians in a day of growing racial tensions, of social isolation, of hatred between employer and employee, of growing trust in violence and doubt in the power of love. They receive help in understanding deviations from normal behavior so that preventive measures may be taken when necessary to protect mental health. It is difficult for an adolescent to keep true to his purpose to live the spiritual life, no matter how vital his church is. The more parents can agree on modes and standards of conduct, the less young people will diverge therefrom.

All of these aspects of sharing will have little meaning unless there is growth taking place in the spiritual lives of the parents, through prayer, in discovering truth, in added knowledge and awareness of God, in living for the will of God. If the True Church is to play its proper part in the spiritual guidance of the child, it must therefore look to the spiritual growth of the parents and others with whom the child lives in the home and the community.

Within its own ministry there are some things the True Church seeks to do directly with persons of all ages. It seeks more time for work and a more effective working use of that time. Moreover, it seeks to become a unit large enough to have adequate equipment and effective leadership. Given a sufficient membership, each local unit of the Church should have a minister to children, one to youth, one to men and women, and a minister of preaching. This implies, of course, ideal conditions. To be most effective, the Church should include all children and young people who go to the same day school. In thousands of communities this means federation of small competing, ineffective churches into one unit sufficiently resourceful to perform the mission of the True Church.

A day nursery for two- and three-year-olds and a kindergarten of four-year-olds are included in the Church program where local conditions indicate the need. If the public school does not provide a kindergarten for five-year-olds, the Church should plan a weekday program for them too. The leaders should be well trained and should be paid for their work if possible, for they are as important as the ministers. These teachers serve not only the child but also his family. Until little churches federate into larger units, they might join in conducting a common nursery and kindergarten. This would be an initial step toward a closer relationship.

For children in the first six grades, the True Church offers at least two-hour sessions on Sunday, plans for some weekday religious instruction and gives additional time for the use of the church building after school hours and on Saturday. It also makes skillful use of the holiday months for this age group, providing for day camps at the church building or at a regular camp site.

Two-hour sessions on Sundays can be scheduled for members of junior high school age. In these sessions the work of the past six years may be brought to a focus in comprehensive, unified instruction in the Bible, and in the resources for the spiritual life, such as prayer, worship, meditation and service; in everyday Christian living; in developing skills of leadership; in coming to a knowledge of and an interest in the world work of the Church. It is at this stage of the child's growth that two years should be set aside for thorough training for membership in the Church. Junior high boys and girls are too often neglected and forgotten. For them there ought also to be gatherings on Sunday and Friday evenings where adequate opportunities are given for crafts and other types of wholesome recreation.

The situation of the senior high school age group is crucial. Its members are now out in the world, bombarded by secularisms, moving in a fellowship that calls to the profane. This is the time when the decision is made to live in the body or in the spirit; to seek the will of God or to bow to the will of the group and the appetites of the flesh; to grow in freedom of the soul or in bondage to the earth. While the roots of these alternatives lie as far back as infancy and childhood, there are no limits to the possibilities the Church faces with youth of this age.

The True Church should be a center of their lives, as the home is a center. They can find in it joy and satisfaction equal to their own vast enthusiasm and energy. The True Church would dip deep into the reservoir of their interest, directing its flow into planning their own worship and conducting the service; into the search for truth and its expression; in forum, over the radio, through choirs and drama. The True Church plans trips to other churches, to jails, to settlement houses, to neglected communities; it provides leadership training; it offers opportunity for service to children and other departments of the Church; it builds up a creative use of leisure through parties, festivals, crafts, arts, music and writing; it suggests social action of many types in which youth may help to make God's will regnant.

Up through the grades, there should be a growing reality as to what is the will of God. Now, at high school age, this knowledge should be vivid and clear to each person, and back of the individual knowledge should be vital group support. At this age, goals of life will be formulated and methods of seeking those goals will be further reduced to habit. These are the words in which one group of high school people came to interpret God's will:

Whatever I do that helps the bodies of all others, and my own, to become healthy and the temple of God's spirit, is doing His will. Whatever I do that helps all whom I meet, and myself, to find the mind of God for our mind, the love of God for all our living, the spirit of Christ for our spirit, is doing the will of God. Whatever I do to build fellowship on that level where persons are encouraged to find union with God in themselves and in others, is doing the will of God.

The senior high age group should be a part of the whole Church. At the end of the eighth grade they should have come into the Church, finding it meaningful to join with adults in the morning worship services. They should be represented in its leadership and have a place in the complete program of the Church. They should have special study opportunities on Sunday. The church building, with supervision, should be open whenever they want it to plan for worship, for fellowship, or for additional study and discussion. There should be a program for them every Saturday evening, planned and led by them with adult help.

In the True Church, the curriculum for high school age members covers all areas of their experience. Its program starts where they are. Its activities center in the church building, in homes, around luncheon tables, in camps. But the fundamental purpose is to lead them into the life of the spirit, into an increasing awareness of God. Failing here, all else is useless.

Beyond the senior high age level, many communities suffer a great loss. Large numbers of their young people go away to college or seek work elsewhere. In such communities, the True Church would build what fellowship it can with those who are left. Churches in college or university communities or in industrial centers have a remarkable opportunity if their programs include more than a preaching ministry. In any event, the True Church follows its young people, keeping in touch with them by letters, by sending copies of sermons, by visits from staff and lay members. Furthermore, the minister sees that other churches in the community to which a young person goes make contact with him.

With these young people, a more personal contact is necessary than with any other group. Life for them is usually becoming more complex. Often they are away from home and need to be enlisted. Away from childhood controls, they need help in forming their own new standards. Those in college face terrific pressures, not the least of which is the power of our sensate culture being brought to bear on them. These are years of battle between early ideals and a new worldliness. These are years of many decisions—on the choice of a mate; on the finding of a job; on the fashioning of a personal, self-determined faith and the abandonment of an inherited one; on the final setting of the sail into God's sea of love or into man's stagnant pool of materialism. Small, informal fellowships hold promise. Letters from a minister have changed many a life. These young people should share with others in a real and vital worship service. There should be a college group fellowship for worship, study, discussion, leadership training and significant service. The amount of time spent together is important but more important still is the quality of the fellowship. Constant support is needed to realize the spiritual goals of life. Retreats under spiritually sensitive leadership offer great opportunity.

The True Church will give much attention to camp programs during vacation periods for junior and senior high and for college groups. No expenditure of time or effort is too large, no financial investment too great. There is no other activity to which the minister can give of his time that will pay greater spiritual dividends.

The ages of twenty-one to thirty-six are usually referred to as "young adult." By thirty-five, in this country, 85 per cent of the people are married. Among those not married there are varying attitudes. For those who intend to work, the vocational choice is made by that time, be it wise or unwise. Thousands of them will be happy simply to have a job. The True Church is concerned primarily with their spiritual ideal; after that, it is interested in the fullest expression of that ideal in all areas of life. While its main purpose is to help each person to seek first the Kingdom of God, it spends its resources of time, leadership and money to help in job-getting, in problem-solving, and in training for all aspects of life.

These young adults are a vital part of the Church. There is an especial need for group fellowship in which they can study and grow into full maturity. There should be a group for men and women meeting occasionally through the week. There should be a Sunday morning study group and a Sunday evening group, all serving as a nucleus of fellowship and discussion. One church I know has organized cells of ten couples. They all report that the only place in which they are encouraged to live by their spiritual ideals is in these cells. They meet monthly for fellowship, study and worship, and plan various service activities for the church and community.

In its ministry to adults, both young and old, the True Church must keep a number of things in mind. There is provision for a variety of worship experiences. A church may have a communion service at 9:00 on Sunday morning; two church services, at 9:30 and 11:00; and a vesper service at 4:00, which is largely musical. On Wednesday night it may have a study group for men and women.

The True Church provides many types of study groups, adjusting their programs to fit the needs of participants. There will be groups of men, of women, and mixed groups, some with large enrollments and others with few, all giving themselves intensively to the spiritual quest. The heart of the True Church's work is to help each person know a growth of God in his soul and to live that realization to the fullest extent. Knowing God in the sanctuary of their souls, these persons go forth to live, making His will known in every walk of life. The secular world, thus, becomes the shadow of the Church.

II

What is the mission of the True Church with those who have not been kept free? Some are earthbound; others are the victims of forces they cannot understand; some have never been awakened. How should the True Church fulfill its mission with these?

A program such as we have just described not only can keep people free and provide a stimulating and guiding fellowship for spiritual growth, but it can at the same time free persons who are enslaved. Let us see, specifically, how this may come about.

Here is another boy, George, conceived and born in love. But the possessive love of a mother kept him dependent, and the critical love of a father imposed prematurely on him adult standards of perfection. The sense of belonging into which he grew was such that he sought refuge in his home instead of accepting it as a port from which to move out into the sea of life. His father was constantly critical of his son, denying him the recognition and the sense of worth that comes from successful functioning. He contrasted George with a younger brother who was more independent and secure. George's ego was hurt; he came to accept his father's verdict that he was slow, that he could not do things as well as Sam, that he could not cope with life. Being thus decompensated, he withdrew within himself. He remained aloof and spent much time alone, avoiding the fellowship of other boys because he felt strange with them. He sought satisfaction in books, in make-believe, in a world of fantasy. His moods drove him to the depths of despair.

The parents appealed to the minister of their church; he went to see George. But the minister's very presence was another confirmation to George that he was a problem. Instead of discussing his problem, however, the minister asked him to go to the church camp. George agreed, just to bring a quick end to an interview that was painful to him. His parents insisted on his going, and some of the young people actually went with him. A girl and boy were assigned to see to it that George found the camp satisfying. He enlisted in planning sessions; he assumed leadership with success and knew for the first time in his life the values of earned recognition. These values he identified with himself. He became more aggressive because he found it satisfying. The minister became his pal, the Church his other home, the youth program his inspiration. He was asked to be co-sponsor of one of the younger youth groups. Gradually he grew. The other sponsor carried him and the group, but always encouraged him. The minister reminded him that he had a destiny; that he had only to believe in God and in himself, if he would love and be loved by others in return. George prayed. He increased in his capacity for participation. He grew in confidence and into a positive outlook.

The next spring he was called into the army. On the last night with his group, they told him of their love for him and their faith in him. As he spoke in reply to them, the inner gates swung open and he became free from the negations that had blocked him. He, too, spoke with love and faith. The minister missed the service, arriving just as the young people were leaving. But as George walked toward him, the minister knew that at last the miracle had happened—George was free from the thought of self that had blocked him from normal human relations. He walked with assurance, revealing a new confidence.

While in the army, he was stationed near a city where he became active in a youth group. There he gave witness and leadership. He began to grow in the spiritual life through prayer, Bible study and thought. He continued to grow in his awareness of God and in faith in himself as a son of God. Out of the service, he is at the present time in the university and is vital and alive in his church and in the spiritual quest.

What set him free? Despite the obstacles in his home that blocked his growth, there were also many good factors. There was a love of God and a deep loyalty to the Church. It was the camp that was the great secret. There his leadership in the youth group and the constant attention of some of the young people and the minister, provided the satisfaction that helped him overcome his habits of withdrawal.

Out of the youth work of this Church have come many similar experiences where youth has found freedom. A girl whose parents were estranged, who failed to make a sorority, who was never sought out by young men, began to seek satisfaction in a make-believe world. She was happy only when she imagined herself to be an actress in a play. She was won to the church group by being enlisted in the dramatic worship services. Boys were confidentially asked to have "dates" with her. She grew in her skill of leadership, until at the end of one youth worship service she said to a member of the group, "Something happened to me. I feel all alive inside." Later, in prayer with the minister, she committed herself to the way of Christ. Today she is still growing.

The True Church can mobilize all available resources for the freeing of young children. It can enlist parents, school leaders and church leaders together. By their own growth in understanding, the child can be set free from compulsions, insecurities, hostilities and other negative impulses.

By freeing one or both parents, the Church can save homes. A husband suffered because of the 1929 stock market crash. He lost his position and sunk to the depths of despair. He had never known God. He lost heart and became drab of soul. His wife, though more sensitive than he, tried to share his "objectivity," seeking to live by the assumption that human intelligence was life's highest good. Hostility and hopelessness grew within the family. At length one of the children, feeling the tension of insecurity, became strained and overactive. The mother could no longer bear the burden. Family life turned to bitterness.

One morning as she listened to a devotional program on the radio, the mother heard a message that called to the denied God within her. The next Sunday the family crossed the city to the church of which the radio speaker was the minister. After the service her husband was skeptical, but the mother felt rewarded. They continued their attendance. Soon he found a position which he still has and now loves. She joined a weekday Bible class and there, over a period of several years, found freedom from all that blocked her from finding union with God. She grew in a great sense of God, in the power to witness for Him to others. By His grace, she found union with her husband in God. Sensing the newness within her and the growing radiance of her life, the father joined an evening study group for men led by one of the laymen. Here he, too, began to grow out of the bondage of his own ego to a full surrender to God and His sovereign will. He has become loving, gentle, radiant and overwhelmingly devoted to his family. Their son, now coming into puberty, is secure and their daughter is happy and free. The wife is one of the key teachers in the church and the husband leads a group dedicated to social Christian action.

A man and woman, both divorced, came to a minister to be married. When the minister inquired whether either was concerned with the divorce of the other, the man asked, "Why?"

"If you were," replied the minister, "I cannot marry you. Divorce," he continued, "is wrong. Jesus speaks plainly on this subject. But if you will study with me until I may become acquainted with you, with your thoughts of each other and of God, I'll consider marrying you."

The man's retort was glib. "We came here to be married, not to study. I have had more experience than you have. I've already been married. Good-by."

As he rose to leave, the woman said, "We will study." They stayed.

Slowly he became co-operative. Gradually the three experienced a rare fellowship as they talked, first of all, of the will of God and of the purpose of creation; then of the quality of life that alone makes true monogamy possible. The two were asked to face the reasons for their failure in their previous marriages. The man frankly declared his full loyalty to sex and his readiness to enjoy it where he could. The woman wanted theirs to be a true marriage. As their study progressed, they both agreed to make right any unfaced wrong with former mates, both of whom were already remarried. With the end of their study, they both accepted Christ as the way to God and joined the church the day of their wedding.

The woman seemed to have known a deep spiritual rebirth. She testified to a newness of life, a peace she had never known, a feeling of rightness through all of living. The man's was a mental acceptance, an incomplete surrender. Although he determined to live by the teachings of Christ, he was cold within—God to him was only a word. He became head of one of the large groups of the church, to which he was faithful and gave effective leadership.

Two years later, one Sunday in the regular service, he had his first deep experience of God. It must have been to him what sun and rain are to the soil of a garden. By his will, his effort of mind, his sincere intent to live by the will of God, he had been enriched. On that Sunday he became free. He had found union with God within his soul.

Another man had lost his job because of his drinking. He became depressed. The minister talked with him, and together they looked at his life and the reasons for his habit. After several interviews, representatives of a unit of Alcoholics Anonymous, which meets in his church building, were sent by the minister to the victim. They worked with him, enlisting him to become a part of their group. Gradually he grew into the very heart of God, becoming free from the tyranny of drink for a full surrender to His will for service to others. He has found a new job and a new life. His house is now a real home, with its inspiration coming from God.

The True Church thus finds that a personal crisis is a doorway to spiritual awakening. A loved one dies; a deep love is rejected; an injustice is wrought; health is lost; moral failure comes. Any one of these may result in a culmination of grief that will drive a person fully to God. Bitterness, defeat or further appeal to the flesh may come again. Or the person under stress may rise temporarily to a high spiritual plane, only to settle back later to the same old level or an even lower one. If it is to last, help must come vividly, guiding him to face and deal positively with the crisis, to find good in it, to make of his cross a crown. Until he has found his own spiritual legs, he needs constant support. The Church must draw on his highest energies with its ministry and help him come, through real prayer, to a day-by-day renewal of eternal life.

The most common and hopeful service the True Church can provide is the freeing not of those who are emotionally blocked, but of those thousands who are merely earthbound, rooted to material things, living only in the body, centered in self, with no higher loyalty than their own ego. That is why, for young people, a camp experience is the most fruitful. For, with most young people who go to camp, money, clothes, bodily pleasures and their own selves are their primary devotion. Here, as they climb Vesper Hill for the first time, they begin to see the immensity of the sky and begin to feel the awe and wonder and mystery of life. The spirit of God in them, heretofore unknown and unheard, now speaks, and they begin to hear. They look about and see others in a new light—not as wearers of clothes nor as attractive dates, but as individuals dignified by the spirit of God. They become interested in truth, they grow thoughtful toward others. When they see a member aloof, they bring him into their fellowship. They learn to sing a new kind of song. They go off, alone and unprompted, to keep vigil with themselves. They give as much money for hungry children in Europe as they spend for candy and ice cream. A new radiance shows in their faces. They have become aware of their own souls and they sense the spirit of God in one another. "This is living," they say. And it is living, living at the very heart of the universe.

When the camp experience is over, all of them do not hold to the newly attained level. Some do; others keep struggling. In so far as their Church is true and realizes its purpose in the home and in the school, they will find it easier to do so. If camps and weekend retreats are a part of the year-round activity of the Church, they are a source of renewed inspiration.

In every sphere of the True Church's activities, be it in the sanctuary, in a study or social action group, in a prayer circle or a radio ministry or a venture in soul-winning, there is always the thrilling possibility that one anchored to the body, bound to the earth, or blocked by some negative impulse, may be led into the life of the spirit. The very hope of it is the inspiration of leadership and the challenge of Christian fellowship. With some it may be sudden; with others, gradual. With some it is a brief glimpse of the Divine; with others, a slow progression toward a long-sought goal. With some it may come as it did to Paul; with others, as Timothy found it. The meeting of a crucial need brings spiritual awakening to some. Loneliness may be healed by true fellowship. A childless couple may be enabled, through the Church, to find a child for adoption. An unsociable individual may be helped to find friendship. A man unemployed may be aided in finding work. Jesus gave men bread, knowing that they needed more than bread. And so the True Church, giving its effort to the solution of earthly problems, awakens its people to the voice of God.

Freedom to grow into the life of the spirit comes in one other way: one who is free helps one who is not free. Like

Christ, he who has been given the lamp of freedom knows his obligation to light the way for those who are lost in the search for the Eternal. No person can remain free and continue to grow spiritually who does not constantly seek to help others share his freedom. One notable place the contemporary Protestant church fails is in winning individuals to the fellowship of Christ. Millions of people who live in cities, towns and rural places are never approached by neighbors who presume to belong to the Church and to love the Lord. Less than half of our population belongs to any church. In our competitive church life, these millions go on unnoticed and unapproached. The fact that thousands do try the contemporary Church, find it wanting and drop out, fails to ruffle the surface of our unchristian complacency.

III

Growth in the life of the spirit results both from man's highest effort of will and discipline and from God's gift of grace. It takes both the effort of man and the gift of God to turn the desert into a blossoming rose. The conflict may be less bitter and the effort of achievement less exacting for one who grew up with a loving attitude than for another who is blocked by hostility, estranged by hatred, and compelled by anger. But the grace of God must be, for both, his inspiration and ultimate reward.

The True Church, drawing upon the resources of religion, psychology and psychiatry, discovers how to lead individuals in the achievement of penitence. Pride insists on the maintenance of self-regard. Pride leads to fear, to dishonesty, to shifting of blame, to mechanisms of escape, to delight in the failure of others. Penitence comes with the miracle of God's forgiveness, and penitence and freedom go hand in hand. Only when one has achieved the penitent spirit can he face himself, seeing his own life with candor and honesty. He achieves it not by yielding to the fear that others will know of his failure, but by yielding to the infinite goodness and glory of God. Only as he comes to know God's mercy can he have mercy. Only as he knows forgiveness, can he truly forgive.

If the individual would know penitence, he must become poor in spirit. But, if his is a sin of commission, the effort to atone and to make restitution, however humbly offered, is only half of penitence. He cannot undo his deed nor cancel his sin. He can only surrender to God. If his sin is one of omission, of refusal or denial, there is no atonement but God's mercy.

To be centered in God is not only to be alive with God's love and to grow in His spirit, but also to translate them into conduct and deed. Knowing God's grace, one is merciful, loving, righteous, ever doing what God wills and what love directs; seeking and sharing truth, helping others find the truth that will make them free.

This achievement of God-centered character, while it is a gift of God's grace to those who live His life among men, is not without struggle. As Harry Cotton, president of McCormick Theological Seminary, says, "To the Christian there is ever the experience of unremitting conflict." An ancient poet sang, "God took the dust of the earth and made man, and God breathed into man the breath of life and man became a living soul." It is from the dual nature of man that the age-old conflict arises. While the flesh cries, "Live in me," aspiration calls, "Rise and reach the spirit of your Maker." Earth demands, "You belong to me," but the sky calls, "You were meant for climbing."

The conflict of the world of things and the life of the spirit is ever present. It is this that keeps the soul vivid, the muscles of the prayer-life strong, and our faith resilient as a tree tried daily by the mountain wind. Constant prayer, daily disciplining, humility of spirit, pureness of heart—these are the elements of victory over self, the approach to peace between man and God.

The stages are plain: to grow from self will to a full surrender to God's will; to achieve penitence and, through it, forgiveness; to cast one's self on God's mercy and center one's thought on His goodness; to translate His ideals into a life of service; to bring Him to life in others; to undergo with strength the unremitting conflict of each day; and to come in time, through the constant discipline of prayer, into the triumphant assurance of God's love.

IV

Translation of spirit into deed—it is the challenge to every individual Christian and to the Church itself. Deeds that keep persons free or liberate them are necessarily individual in effect. But deeds that help create, support and sustain community living on a Christian level have both individual and social significance. The spirit is both one and many.

While it is apparent that Jesus put chief emphasis on freeing the individual, it is also clear that he was concerned with the social order as it affected the individual, that he assailed systems that blocked people, that blight and hurt them, that exploited them. The True Church, in its local units and its collective action, enlists and trains and energizes its membership for constant participation in building the beloved community which is its aim. Itself a beloved community, the True Church is concerned with bringing every geographic community, large and small, within the bounds of a vast, universal community of love. But prefatory to assuming this concern, the Church must make sure that it actually is, in all its operations, the beloved community—that it is, in short, the kind of community which it asks others to emulate: a community without breaches caused by economic differences, without racial differences, without creedal differences.

The local church, working as a unit or joined with other churches and other agencies, seeks to build a beloved community within the family, the school and in every type of community life. While it does not seek to dominate the collective will that is the government, it does aim to send into the leadership of government those who "do justly, show mercy and walk humbly before God." The Church, in its local units and in its collective might, rises up against any exploitation of persons, any inequality that robs the individual of his rights and opportunities in order that a few may have the advantage. The Church attempts to preserve those relationships that give the greatest freedom to live by God's will for the good of all men, and opposes any forces or institutions that abuse freedom or withhold it from any person or group of persons.

On national and international levels, the True Church must speak with a united and collective voice. While the Federal Council of Churches, the World Council of Churches and similar agencies, such as the International Council of Religious Education, are effective and powerful, it is imperative that these mighty interdenominational agencies hasten their purpose to unify and that the Protestant denominations unite in carrying out a clear-cut program. The development of this program should include: (1) Strengthening the local units of the Church; (2) supplying new types of professional leadership for all phases of its new ministry; (3) pooling of its re-sources to provide more effective supervision and training; (4) building of a new seminary to train the new minister for the new Church; (5) building some outstanding Christian colleges and professional schools; (6) pooling of its resources for a more effective use of the radio and the printing press. These are positive and fundamental actions the Church cannot wait to take. It needs a united voice to carry on effectively a constructive program dealing with the areas of tension in our national and world life.

In so far as the Protestant church can co-operate with the two branches of the Catholic church—Roman and Eastern—and also with the Jewish leaders, this should emphatically be done. Every conceivable effort ought to be made for united action. At this moment the racial issue trembles to be faced and solved. If America stands for Christian world leadership, we must deal with the racial issue on Christ's basis. The Church must go as far as science at least. If the Church hedges on this issue, it has indeed become emasculated and its talk of brotherhood is a mockery.

The clash between capital and labor is a conflict of mighty forces, and in its issue is the threat of fascism on the one hand, of communism on the other. No one can doubt the influence of communism within the labor unions. It is a terrific and tremendous challenge to the Church to see that we keep our freedom and, at the same time, that labor, capital and agriculture dedicate themselves to the interests of all our people. If we are to keep our way of life, we must fashion our economy so as to provide full employment for all, and our social structure so as to give greater equality of opportunity for all. The constant and imperative challenge is to make our collective will, our elected government, function effectively and honestly, being sensitive to the valid claims of pressure groups and yet acting for the best interests of all. If the spirit of God moves within us, it will move us in these directions. The question for the Church to answer is whether we have any right to expect our national government, the voice of our collective will, to be any better than the individual component voices that make it up. Our government will be no more righteous than are we.

In our international relations there is now the challenge, once and for all, to build one world if there is to be any world. Every resource that can be brought to bear in this direction will be far from enough. Each local unit of the True Church must contribute as much money for rehabilitation and sending forth the message of Christ as it spends on itself. Food, clothing and workers in the spirit of Christ must be sent to all nations. We must bring, or help to bring, some of the key people of other nations to live among us here. The True Church seeks to send into all aspects of world government men and women sensitive to the will of God.

In approaching the correction of the social and economic system within our own country we find ourselves facing very complex problems. In 1870 47 per cent of the gainfully occupied in the United States were farmers or farm laborers. By 1940 this percentage had fallen to 17 per cent. Wage earners and white collar workers had increased from 37 per cent to 61 per cent. More and more people live in large cities today. More and more people work in large establishments of one kind or another. Complexities such as these will not grow fewer. We must remind ourselves that freedom and democracy can survive only by a positive program of action firmly based on the broad education and understanding of our whole population, and on their active and self-disciplined participation in the formation of a national policy.

Participation—the right kind of participation—will come more easily and with greater strength when the Church assumes its proper role of weaving into the fabric of our life the will of God. Never have we needed so much to increase in wisdom, and in stature and favor with God and man. Only in so far as our people have the opportunity and the basic necessities to win health of body and mind, is there hope that they will grow into that higher level of spiritual insight and reality where they find union with God in themselves, and the union with God in others that is the basis of world brotherhood.

The facts of our common life make it clear that we are now in an era in the history of man marked by the passing of a social system. Uncontrolled industrial capitalism, upon which the structure of the civilization of the West was built, is crumbling. It can no longer sustain itself, much less bear the burden of the world. The True Church utilizes the lessons of history not only in the quest of the spirit but also in the economic quest. Social systems flourish and in time decay and die because they fail to support man in the fulfillment of his divine destiny. Once it was the agricultural imperialism of Rome, which, after hundreds of years of power, decayed into the blackness of the Dark Ages. Out of that darkness rose feudalism, which fashioned the ways of men for five hundred years and which, with all its ills, gave us the Gothic cathedrals and the medieval universities. But feudalism, too, began to rust away. Gradually, throughout the Renaissance and the Reformation and many years of religious wars, the industrial age of *laissez faire* and the capitalism which created these modern times came into power.

Why is industrial capitalism failing? Because it is not in harmony with God's moral design, with His will that leads to humility, justice and mercy, the mad passion for profit has emasculated our government so that it, like business, is run for the welfare of a part of our population. The system exploits labor for the purposes of private profit, as surely as Rome exploited the slave and feudalism the serf. There are differences in the means used but the end is the same. Labor is now organized and between it and capital there is an impasse. One of three solutions will result: fascism, communism, or a growth of our collective will toward an expanded government equipped to control and use our resources to meet the basic needs of life for the good of all. It is a change which will demand leaders of government sensitive to God's leadership. It means, too, that those individuals and corporations which continue to control the means of a livelihood for the worker must make loyalty to God's will the rule of life. Without this, no system will work.

"This is the time to outlaw war," General Douglas MacArthur said recently. This is the time for a mighty peace offensive. There is no doubt that the United Nation charter and organization mark the farthest advance the nations of the world have ever made in finding a way to work together peaceably and to solve their differences on a nonviolent basis. The Church faces the challenge to persuade people to disarm their hearts. It faces the challenge of bringing people to accept the moral order of love, the very principle upon which the universe is based. At this moment, America is in a better position than is any other nation to lead a mighty peace offensive, to help all nations find bread, and to help all people find a creed to live by.

This involves adult education for which the church is one of the most hopeful agencies. If ministers grow beyond the thought of occupying the pulpit as their major function and seize the possibilities of adult education within the program of the Church, if the Church joins in working with other agencies in the community, and if all of the denominations learn to pool their resources nationally and on a world basis, then we have a real opportunity to lay the foundation for peace. He who believes in the Kingdom of God must hold that that Kingdom must prevail upon earth. The only God possible is a God whose will determines the affairs of men.

III ⟿

IT USES HOLY RESOURCES

IN THE preceding chapter we have observed the process by which the True Church must develop its ministry—a ministry which aims to stimulate and guide the growth of the spiritual life in personal and collective relations. How that aim is achieved is a major concern of the True Church. The emphasis is not on teaching the content of this many pages of the Bible or of that many pages of church history. The Church is not primarily a merchant of facts, a dispenser of books, an agency to tell persons what or how to think. Its purpose is to light the candle of the Lord in each person. It enlightens the mind by first stimulating the desire to be enlightened.

The Bible has the same vital importance as does any rich body of source material. But only in so far as it is intelligently interpreted, is it helpful to spiritual growth. There is need for words and ideas, for strategies and techniques illustrated through parable and analogy; for music, drama and story; for beauty and color; for a knowledge of the agelong progress in man's response to God's revealing. These are not, however, the primary concern of the True Church. The center of that concern is the individual, the growth of his soul, and the contribution of his living to the spiritual growth of others. Whatever helps to achieve it—whether Biblical literature or scientific data or a work of art—is a holy resource.

The True Church declares that no man ever reached a spiritual level of living through the verbal expression of scripture,.

59

by using religious terms, or repeating words in prayer. Did not Jesus tell us that all who say, "Lord, Lord!" will not enter into the Kingdom of God? Only when worship opens the spirit to a fuller incarnation of God, a deeper sovereignty of the Divine, a greater sense of oneness with God and with all humanity, does it serve its purpose. The insight of worship is not complete until it results in personal union with God, union with God in others, and in a manifestation of God's will to others. One has truly worshiped when, in his relationship with others, they, too grow in an awareness of God. When he is sensitive to those near and far, sensitive to the point of giving and sharing and loving, then religion has accomplished its end and the True Church is really manifest.

In Ezekiel 33:32 we read, " . . . for they hear thy words, but they do them not." There is nothing to indicate that these enthusiastic churchgoers to whom Ezekiel spoke were hypocritical. They heard the words, they loved the music, they were devoted to the beauty of ritual, they listened to the prophet speak of life, of God, of duty, and must have gone away feeling more secure in God's world. Life for them had doubtless taken on greater proportions—they felt themselves no longer to be orphaned but the favorite sons of the Most High. Yet they continued living by their own self-esteem, devoted to self and materialism, forgetting God. The words of God, the music, the symbols, the beauty were a temporary stimulant or escape, but their lives remained basically unchanged. They did not grow Godward.

Two things—perilous both—often happen in the contemporary Church when people listen to religious truth. First, the very talk about ideals and obligations and dedications, their exaltation in litany and song and sermon, frequently become a substitute for true devotion. Listeners who believe they are absorbed in worship are too frequently only inflated with emotion. The church member who leads children in a twenty-minute worship service does not thereby demonstrate a constant realization of God's guidance in life and a growing sense of awareness of Him. Nor is memorizing ten verses of scripture a substitute for practicing them day by day. And there is a well-known tendency even among the most devout, to postpone doing the deed, carrying out the inspiration, launching the spiritual quest, growing in the prayer life, seeking to free others, fostering a crusade.

The proper emphasis, then, is on the processes by which the Divine influence grows in individual and collective lives, and by which God's Kingdom comes into all areas of community living —locally, nationally and on a world scale. These have already been discussed. Let us consider next the resources which the True Church uses to this end.

I

The True Church makes major use of the resource of fellowship. We have been thinking of the Church as a fellowship of the way. Personality, in a real sense, is one of the products of social interaction. It is that which draws a baby to its parents and they to it. It is that which draws a girl to her group, a boy to his gang, and that, in due season, which leads a man and a woman together in love. The level on which this fellowship is achieved is highly important and obviously is determined by the level on which those who share that fellowship are living. It may be on a low level where the individual loses identity in a collectivized mass, where God is denied and the worst in man is brought out. It may be on a level where only physical nearness is achieved. Thousands of marriages are nothing more than the union of two bodies, never culminating in companionship of the soul. Spiritually the two never become one.

The True Church is a fellowship. And this fellowship is an essential resource of the Church. Wherever there are people bound together in the name of the True Church, that fellowship is re-created over and over again, and its members grow in God-awareness within themselves and with one another. The early Christian communities at Corinth, Ephesus, Thessalonia and Rome must have been like this. Fellowship is always the basis of the True Church, so that persons may find support in one another for growth in the life of the spirit.

In its use of fellowship as a holy resource, the True Church considers the fellowship of a party as sacred in significance as the fellowship of worship. The criterion is that people grow akin on a level of their best. The Church sponsors its own social gatherings with this end in view, knowing that in such gatherings each person learns compatibility and grows into a feeling of belonging to the group. In the same way, the True Church looks upon a hike for a group of children as an important activity, as a primary step toward its ultimate aim. It recognizes that guiding a group of children in planning a worship center or in planning for the experience of worship lays the foundation for the growth of a kinship that will make actual worship more meaningful and real. It looks upon a craft, drama or creative play group as a holy fellowship in which the individual learns to create values and know communion. Here fellowship has a new quality which enables the person to live creatively when alone.

The True Church may, with wisdom, choose a group of men, not at the moment residing at the heart of the sanctuary, to plan the budget and execute its financial campaign. A few years later these men will have grown in the life of prayer and in a sense of God's will so that they are ready to serve as deacons, or as participants in other aspects of a reciprocal ministry. The first step in the spiritual growth of many a boy has been taken when he engaged in some seemingly trivial activity of a group project. Such an experience may be the start in the direction of God. All activities of the True Church have one fundamental purpose: to help people grow in union with God within themselves and with one another; to provide fellowship to support them in the spiritual quest; and to enlist their best efforts both to the fellowship and to the fulfilling of God's purpose in life. The relation between the inner spirit and outer environment is one of mutual interaction. The spirit motivates the body, but proper social conditions can often induce the religious spirit in the individual, who in other circumstances would be without it.

The True Church is always alert to recognize and appreciate fellowships other than its own which share its aims. It welcomes and makes use of any group where, without reference to race, color or creed, love for God and for fellow man is supreme. The True Church also reaches beyond the limits of time to find bonds of communion with those of past ages whose spirits are a part of the glorious fellowship. And, surmounting geographic obstacles, it brings within its brotherhood all those over the world who have surrendered to God's will and who constitute the universal Church. It can muster resources from all time and space and focus them at the spot where they are needed.

II

The Holy Bible is a major resource. It is a record of God's self-disclosure to man through his experiences in many walks of life. It was imparted in the midst of the events of war and peace and under the diversified influences of political, economic and social life. In a sense it might be regarded as the autobiography of the human race through the stages of infancy, youth, adolescence and manhood. It is a drama of human life —a drama of glory when men responded to the Divine and a drama of tragedy when human devices disregarded or ignored the manifest will of God. Viewed as history, the Bible has a continuity of thought with a steady progression toward perfection.

Just as any narrative is held together by its central theme, the Bible depends for its unity on a continuous faith in God which inspired its divers authors. The historians, biographers, dramatists, poets and letter writers who produced it sought to put down in words their own experience of God, through which they came to Life Eternal. All of them were impelled by the supreme purpose of bearing testimony to the guidance and deliverance of the wise and gracious Providence. The message of the gospels, though as old in existence as the foundations of the world, though amplified and made plain from time to time by the devotees of all religions, by saints, seers and prophets in every age, yet reached its highest expression and richest form in the words of the prophets and of the New Testament. These writers were not literary purists. They were men of deep religious concern, men who wrote of things as they saw them in the light of what they knew to be Eternal realities. It is the passion of God which is unfolded in the Bible. Through its pages runs the thread of an unblemished hope for the eventual establishment of the reign of God in each human life and in the expression of collective human will.

The Christian Bible is truly the unequaled manual of religious devotion. Its promises of fellowship with God, its varied directions for the performance of duty, its many-sided programs for the guidance of the individual and society, its unlimited resources for realizing the Divine purpose of living, have quickened the hearts and restored the hope of millions. The essential value of the Bible lies in its ability to encourage every individual to enter the sanctuary of personal communion with God to receive a vivid sense of the Divine presence in daily living.

It is a record covering twelve hundred years of spiritual searching for God, culminating in The Sermon on the Mount. In those words of Christ is the true pattern for living, the means of coming into the fullest life of the spirit, the way to Life Eternal. It is the Eternal Gospel. The Church must excite persons with a passion to achieve the Life and the Love that is the will of God in order to lead them beyond a mere knowledge of the scriptures into an incorporation of this knowledge within the plan and pattern of their living. When this is achieved, the Bible becomes a Book of Life. Alone, the Bible is the True Church's first source of inspiration and its major guide to living. Applied to the processes of activity, the insights of the Bible give them new meaning and added significance.

In addition to the scriptures, the True Church makes use of devotional literature, including music and art of the Christian religion and of other religions. It seeks to help each person use them as means and sources of inspiration, as bread for his soul, as grist for his mind, as oxygen for the lungs of his spirit. These offer to the individual not a substitute for thinking but a stimulus and aid. The Church bids each of its members to make the experience of all others his own.

The True Church also makes extensive use of the resources of the arts, philosophy and science, grading them according to the age and perception of the learner. It uses the resources of economics, political economy and the social sciences, and of many other fields of knowledge, drawing upon all to give the individual a better understanding of God's many-faceted world.

III

Another holy resource is that of beauty. Kirby Page has given us a glimpse of its possibilities:

The surpassing beauty of a sunset should not only be enjoyed, it should be recognized as the handiwork of God. A person can train himself to such a degree that sensitiveness to the glories of nature automatically brings God into mind. Nature in its myriad forms of beauty should ever be recognized; the awe-inspiring majesty of the starry firmament; the indescribable blending of color at dawn; the sinking of a flaming ball of fire into the horizon at sunset; fleecy clouds floating through the heavens; fog, rain, snow, rhododendrons, poppies, roses; an orchard at blossomtime; silvery reflections on a calm lake lined with green trees; the resistless onward surge of a mighty river; the raging torrent of a mountain stream; the reverent silence of majestic trees.

It is good for the spirit of man to experience beauty:

Here is peace and loveliness ever mingled:
Organ music of winds and birds and branches,
And a brooding Presence that makes each moment
A benediction.

Music is a window to fuller life. Harmony stirs the soul of man, quickens imagination, heightens aspiration, and forges determination. Wise is the individual who arranges his time with hours for great music and who has trained the faculty of recognition, recognition of harmony as a revelation of God. Carl Sandburg tells of the man who went to a concert tired and discouraged and who came away transformed: "When he got outside his heels hit the sidewalk a new way. He was the same man in the same world as before. Only there was a singing fire and a climb of roses everlastingly over the world he looked on."[1]

These resources of beauty are limitless and are used with power by the True Church.

IV

Another resource that the True Church employs is the knowledge gained by psychology and psychotherapy. No science has undergone such a revision as psychology. Having outgrown its former narrow emphasis on measurements and physiological conditions, psychology has developed into a study of the total aspect of human behavior. Modern psychology is based on the fundamental tendencies of the organism as integrated in a complex society. Today it seeks to discover how the mind works, its relation to the environment, and the relation of the environment to the mind. The major change in psychology has been a shift from understanding the individual as a person apart to understanding him as a functioning unit in the whole. There has been a growing emphasis on the study of the group to the point that there is no longer a dividing line between personal and social psychology, providing a tool thereby which the Church can use for its purposes.

It is interesting to note that with this expansion in the field of psychology, there has been accompanying growth in the idea of personality. In his book, *Jesus and Human Personality*, Albert Day has an interesting concept of personality. He speaks of the person at birth as being a raw self with capacities, potentialities, possibilities. He thinks of personality as the goal toward which that raw self is constantly growing and developing. Gordon

[1] From *Motive* magazine, April, 1946. Used with permission.

Allport in his book, *Personality*, gives this definition: "Personality is the dynamic organization within the individual of those psycho-physical systems that determine his unique adjustments to his environment." Personality is defined as the sum total of all of our attitudes by another authority, George H. Preston, in his book, *Psychiatry for the Curious*.

The growth of the concept of psychology and of personality not only brings the function of the psychologist and the psychiatrist closer together but also brings their work more and more into the very heart of the process to which the True Church is dedicated. A leader within the True Church consequently needs to understand the insights of psychology and the skills of psychotherapy as well as to work with the specialists within these fields.

The total personality is a function of a socio-psycho-biologic unity in a given setting at a given time and can be understood only if studied as such. These given elements must be studied with reference to one another. Personality is a complex whole responding to, being conditioned by, determining as well as being determined by the environment. Actually, literally, there are no rugged individualists—every person is a part of the social whole and the whole modifies and changes the form of the parts. As one grows in the God-mind, he comes naturally to a realization of his oneness with all humanity.

Parallel with psychology, personal ministry has been undergoing a fundamental change of interpretation. While counseling is as old as Christianity—Jesus was one of the most effective counselors in the history of the world—it has not been so effectively used in the Western world partly because of our addiction to mass processes and partly due to the authoritarian emphasis in the Church and school. We could spend a good deal of time at this point discussing the various emphases that educational procedure has undergone. There was a time when it was thought that education was a matter of providing the person with the right facts and ideas. But Freud and others after him have made clear to us that simply knowing the truth is not enough. One must be free from both conscious and unconscious forces in his deepest mind in order to apply the truth which he acquires. It is not enough for a person to know. He must feel at ease with his knowledge.

In public education and in the Church we have shifted gradually from the content-centered to the life-centered emphasis. But the training of our teachers, unfortunately, has not kept abreast of this shift. Few teachers know how to start where a single learner is and help him grow from that point; few teachers know how to start where a group of learners are and guide them from that point. Consequently, a body of knowledge is imposed upon a learner; his selection is made for him. A system of facts and a body of data which may not be fundamentally vital to his life are thrust upon him, making him dependent on a type of rote learning rather than freeing him for independent thinking.

During the past fifty years there has been a growing emphasis on counseling, where leader and individual share together in person-to-person relationships. Freud contributed his emphasis on the deeper therapy that seeks to free the individual from blocks that prevent his continued growth. Psychoanalysis was an accepted emphasis for a time and is still a vital aspect of psychotherapy. But it is only one aspect, for now we have added group therapy, recreational therapy, the therapy of creative fellowship, and dramatic psychotherapy.

There has been a marked development in group counseling

as well as individual counseling. There is now evidence that it is possible to counsel through the lecture or sermon, through drama and group discussion. Some ministers are finding that a sermon will many times free a person from a block that prevents his growth, and will give him the readiness to deal with his own situation or to join with another person in asking help of the psychotherapist. Or life itself may provide the readiness to face the need, as when crises come.

The concept of counseling has grown far beyond the mere business of giving advice, of approving or forbidding. It has grown away from the ideas of command and suggestion into the larger concept of helping a person to gain and to maintain freedom for growth. Carl Rogers in his book *Counseling and Psychotherapy*, has given unique help in making clear this interpretation, though it is interesting to see in Gordon Gardner's book, *Human Relations in Industry*, his discovery of the validity of the nondirectional emphasis in counseling. In the writer's experience there has often been a place for suggestion—that is, the therapist can often shorten the course of counseling without interfering with the process of freeing the person.

A medical officer of the local draft board sent me a man who was determined to commit suicide if he were inducted. He arrived in a high state of excitement. He showed panic and indications of a feeling of guilt. One could have talked endlessly against self-destruction to no avail—the probable result to the man would have been suicide or the development of some type of escapist mental illness. However, in an hour and a half we two got to the real point of the trouble. To have followed the nondirectional technique might have taken as many as a dozen sessions; yet in that hour and a half none of the principles of psychotherapy were violated. As the conference progressed, I foresaw what the problem was, but did not point it out. Instead the young man was directed to speak openly of the difficulty. Once the fear was out in the open, I was able to lead him to see the truth, and to help him find evidence that the only injury that could come from the habit he confessed would result from anxiety. We both worked out a program of thinking which proved, in subsequent weeks, to be effective. This program included an acceptance of forgiveness, evidence from authorities he trusted that there was no reason for permanent physical injury, and assurance that he was free to live a normal life. He was helped to find in prayer a source of personal power and peace. He was helped to see that atonement was not enough, that the important thing for him was to grow. Incidentally, in this situation we can see that knowledge and facts were not enough. Concommitant emotions had to be dealt with. It is also perfectly plain that advice and inspirational talks alone would not have helped. Counselor and counseled needed, together, to find the source of the emotional disturbance, bring it out in the open, and work out a program of release and help. Subsequent letters from the young man have proven that the outcome was favorable.

It is not possible within the confines of this book to discuss further the techniques of counseling and the utilization of the resources of psychotherapy. Let it suffice to say that the minister needs to understand the principles of counseling in person-to-person relations, in group guidance, and in guidance through the lecture or sermon. The minister must also be skilled in training others in counseling. He needs training in working with the physician and with the psychiatrist. The True Church is the most fundamental agency in the community for the growth and preservation of mental health. Religion at its best is the only true psychiatry.

The minister needs to recognize the signs of mental illness

and the behavior mechanisms that need redirection. When we survey the field of mental pathology, it is evident that the difference between normal people and those mentally afflicted is often apparently slight. The line between normal and abnormal is frequently not clearly drawn. For our purposes here, it is unnecessary to go into detail, but will suffice to discuss briefly the main classes of mental diseases. This will enable us to see how behavior mechanisms often lead to mental ailments.

One class of mental disease includes types which rest on a distinctly organic basis.[2] These embrace psychoses with brain infections and psychoses with senile or arteriosclerosis accompaniments; psychoses resulting from the toxic effects of alcohol, drugs or metals, from the poisons of general infections, or from exhaustion; psychoses due to such diseases as pellagra, pernicious anemia or endocrine deficiencies; and finally, psychoses caused by the damage of tumors. Obviously the minister is incapable of coping with such conditions. The most he can do is to arrange for competent care.

Then there is the widely misunderstood class known as psychoneurosis. Other terms used synonymously for psychoneurosis are nervousness, nervous breakdown, nervous exhaustion. Persons who are psychoneurotic retain in great measure a normal orientation to life. In this classification are included such conditions as phobias, that is, fears not based on reason and not consistent with facts. In addition there are the so-called compulsive neuroses, associated with or representative of obsessions. The obsession may center about some such incident of behavior as keeping clean. I once dealt with a boy who was compelled to wash some thousands of times, it seemed, after he

[2] The following description of the classes of mental illness appears in *The Church and the Returning Soldier*, pp. 116-125.

had been in contact with any possible sort of dirt. The compulsion dated from a time when he wanted to stop school and was disallowed to do so by his parents. He always got himself dirty at ten o'clock at night, and by the time ablutions were complete, everybody in the family was too tired to get up early enough for him to go to school. Yet the trick survived the need it was intended to serve, and the fear of being sent to school was transferred to the means that got him out of it. Compulsions are usually associated with various fears. These may start from normal sources, but they grow to psychopathic dimensions. Then they have passed beyond voluntary control. Sometimes obsessions are quite harmless in appearance, such as the constant running through one's mind of certain tunes, or the recurrence of such queries as, did I turn the automobile lights off?

A third class of mental illness is known as manic-depressive psychosis. Those whose ailments fall in this category have moods that swing from deep depression to high elation. The manic-depressive becomes so submerged in anxiety as to lose all possibility of satisfaction in ordinary life. At such times there exists a real danger of self-destruction. When the mood of elevation reaches high altitude, there is also danger that he may lose good judgment. The patient becomes unrestrainedly reckless. He may spend all the money he has in hand and mortgage his future in the bargain.

A fourth class is known as schizophrenia. This disease was formerly called dementia praecox, often expressed more popularly as "personality splitting." Here, for example, is a young man whose sister was adopted. The adopted girl came first, he was born later. The girl was easily controlled but the boy had a mind of his own. The result was that the parents compared him with his sister very unfavorably. The contrast did him great injury, and he sought refuge in a world of fantasy where he imagined he was someone else. His teachers, sensing delusional tendencies, enlisted the help of a minister who had some psychiatric background, and with the co-operation of the parents a program of correction was planned. The boy has since come to find normal compensation in his own name and in his own personality; he has learned to adapt himself to his school and his Church. He undoubtedly will be saved from further mental symptoms.

Finally, there is the psychopathic personality. Psychopaths act out their maladjustment conflicts in antisocial behavior instead of developing symptoms. As a rule they lack adequate social values. They are devoid of any sense of responsibility. They are seemingly unable to benefit by their experience and the trait of disloyalty characterizes all their relationships. In this group fall the out-and-out criminals, most of whom are of a pronounced neurotic type. Besides these, there is the parasitic personality who feels inadequate, dependent, helpless. With the parasite is classed the person who suffers from a mother complex, which a man sometimes may transfer from his mother to his wife, whom he punishes for his own dependency. In this group, too, are included the inveterate liar, the thief, the alcoholic.

In the True Church the minister is not only aware of various types of mental illness, but works closely with the physician in discovering them and in helping the afflicted to get treatment. In addition, it is important that the minister and his assistants be sensitive to those deviations from the normal which are common among most people. The healthy mind is one that faces all the facts in a situation and then comes to a decision or course of action without regard to the cost. The so-called conscious mind and unconscious mind are basically one. But when a mind is abnormal, it adopts roundabout methods to reach a desired end. The link between the conscious and the unconscious which facilitates the transfer between the two may be interrupted or severed. This may result from an effort to compensate, to conceal deficiencies in one range by assuming superiority in another. We are all familiar with the ways whereby one tries to compensate for suspected inferiority. A common expedient is to assume the role of the bully, to be dogmatic, loud, boisterous, cocksure. This type is easily recognized.

Sometimes a person, feeling inferior, will compensate by setting high and unattainable goals. Then he will wax critical of others for their failure to reach these goals, apparently wholly unaware that he cannot reach them himself. Or he will erect a system of delusions, imagining he is some other person. People who are dissatisfied with life often flee into a world of fancy where they become someone else. When the effort to find compensation proceeds to this length, the patient is deranged and would be diagnosed as a schizophrenic. More normal forms of compensation are seen in such cases as a boy who is deficient in his studies trying to excel in athletics, or as another who is weak physically striving to become a master in intellectual fields.

A degree of compensation may be normal and wholesome. But the healthy approach consists in beginning where one is and making the most of what one has, utilizing all available resources of religion, of knowledge, and of friendship. The world is full of men and women who are heroes and heroines because they do little things in a big way.

Another type of mind that is off balance is the rationalizing mind. One rationalizes when he uses reason to support an idea or mode of conduct that is emotionally determined. Suppose a child is tardy at Sunday school. The teacher asks why, and if the child were to tell the truth, his reply might be: "I hate Sunday school and take as long as I can to get here." Or if the teacher were to ask the parent, the truth might sound like this: "Frankly, I just don't think it's too important." But instead of this, the child blames his tardiness on his mother or the clock being late, and the parent makes excuses about not being able to start the car. Rationalization stems from the fact that when one begins to feel that he has been motivated too much by selfish impulses, he tries to escape reproach. The assigned motives are better than the real ones.

One of the interesting things about rationalization is that it detracts attention from the cause and effect behind the reasoning process itself. A wife asks her husband to wash the windows and he suddenly develops a sore throat. By this act, the husband feels he can divert his wife's attention from the fact that he does not want to wash the windows to the fact that he has a sore throat. A certain amount of rationalization enters into every person's behavior. Its chief danger lies in the victim's learning to deceive himself too effectively. A person can get to the place where the delusion is so strong that he cannot tell the real from the unreal, the true from the false.

Another interesting deviation of the mind which is off normal is sometimes called projection. Projection is the attempt by an individual to assign to other people or even to inanimate objects, attributes that are really his own qualities, but which he fails or refuses to acknowledge in himself. Thus critics of gossipers may be gossips themselves. Snobs are usually impatient with other snobs. The self-righteous accusers who proposed to stone the woman taken in adultery were probably guilty of the same offense, as Jesus readily surmised. Two common traits resulting from projection are faultfinding and shifting the blame. Both represent efforts to save oneself the embarrassment of recognizing his personal shortcomings. This type of deviation has a great deal in common with the alcoholic. Its effect being to soothe, one resorts to it constantly. Or one may seek comfort in the idea that he is being persecuted, and that a hostile world is deliberately keeping him from doing what his talents entitle him to do.

In more extreme cases the mental victim may revert to the status of the infant and evade the problems of adult life by reproducing his life as a child. This involves acting emotionally rather than rationally. Though a full-grown man, the patient pouts in the face of criticism, cries over his failures, employs baby talk when excited to anger or frustration. Many of us have seen a golfer throw his bag of irons into the water when the ball lands in the lake; a hunter break his gun when he misses his shot; a motorist kick his car when the engine balks. All such persons are behaving in a way appropriate to a child in the nursery. They revert to the childish behavior their age might lead one to expect they had put away. Bodily injury, undoubtedly, may result from this type of conduct. Digestive processes are inhibited, arteries constrict, an undue load is placed on the heart, and the entire system is poisoned and impaired.

A further type of abnormal reaction is sometimes called identification. This is the effort to claim, as one's own, qualities which in reality belong to others. A boy may insist on wearing glasses because his best friend wears them. All would agree that identification has a beneficent aspect. It helps one expand beyond the borders of self. But it is dangerous when it leads to fantasy. If it results in a morbid extreme of hero worship, then it weakens personality rather than strengthens it. If it confuses the real with the unreal, or eventuates in slavish imitation, it robs the person of what is inalienably his own.

The mind becomes clearly unhealthy when mental conflict issues in physical symptoms. Disabilities, at first feigned to provide an excuse for failure or to excite sympathy and attention, actually become real. A person may become as ill as he says he is or wishes he might be. His body takes him at his word, and the headache which was designed to justify his staying in bed an extra hour in the morning may finally keep him there all day.

A program of emotional education from birth up through the various stages of the individual's life is very important. If all of the emphases included in the foregoing chapter are adequately made, then this will naturally follow.

The minister and physician should work together. Oftentimes the minister can influence people to go to the physician when they need him. Where there is a nervous condition, any type of depression or panic, the first step the minister takes is to get the person to a reliable physician for a physical checkup. If a child is retarded or overstimulated, similar steps must be taken. A girl with an I.Q. of 110 was failing in her school work. When the minister was called in by her mother and the school principal, his first question was, "Has she been to a physician recently?" The answer was in the affirmative. However, even after being freed from an emotional hurt caused by the unfavorable contrast of the girl with a younger, more attractive sister, she still did not make the progress in school which she should have made. The minister asked that the physician be called in again. In the light of all the facts, the doctor decided that a metabolism test should be given. It was found that the girl's metabolic rating was minus 35. After proper treatment, she advanced from the level of failure to a B average in the space of three months.

This is an interesting illustration of the co-operation possible between school and home, between church and physician. Similar teamwork is possible in premarital counseling, in marital difficulties, in cases of reconversion hysteria, and in cases of anxieties where the person focuses attention on physical symptoms. Often the minister can be of great resource in preparing highly emotional people for the experience of entering a hospital to undergo surgery. The True Church can be helpful in situations where psychosomatic medicine is indicated.

In a more fundamental sense, the True Church would be helpful in the areas of prevention and of construction in programs of health education. The means of accomplishment may be through teaching that keeps thinking positive and that results in faith banishing fear; through religious growth that achieves the acceptance of forgiveness; or through the growth of love that banishes hate. If a person becomes mentally ill, the minister can be of assistance in directing him to a psychiatrist, and in getting the members of his family to approve treatment in a mental hospital if that becomes necessary. A positive program of any unit of the True Church helps people deal with minor types of mental illness, and a positive program of mental hygiene will keep people mentally well. If the minister is aware of the signs of mental illness and can help his people become aware of them, they will seek help when needed before the problem becomes too serious, eliminating the possibility of self inflicted damage to others.

In one church I know of there has been only a single onset of schizophrenia in ten years. Not one case of involutional melancholia in a membership of over twelve hundred families has arisen in two years in that parish. There have been only two cases of manic-depressive psychoses among the men during that period, and with 637 men and women in the armed services, not one was discharged as a psychoneurotic and not one failed emotionally during the period of service. This record seems to prove the worth of making co-operative use of the resources of religion, psychology, psychotherapy and medicine.

V.

The Church should use the resources of the school, social agencies, libraries, courts and all other organizations which give their efforts to the constructive direction of growing life. The True Church maintains close relationship with the schools, there being constant co-operation between the leaders in the school, parents and leaders in the Church. Church and school leaders also work together in the interest of those children who lack security or need specific help. When a child gets into difficulty and is called into juvenile court, the court and the Church join forces. It has been the experience of one minister that more than one hundred boys and girls have been put into the custody of their parents with responsibility only to him. In only one instance was there failure to help the child find security and make a helpful adjustment. The Church and police work together with parents, helping their children achieve the maximum in growth. When a wrong has been committed, punishment may be exacted or fines may be levied, but it is done not to hurt the offender but to assist in his growth.

In giving help to families in need of additional financial resources, in problem-solving, in securing work, in facing severe crises, the Church and social agencies also work together. These agencies are another expression of the Church in action. The closer the Church works with them, the more their incentive may carry with it the fullest spiritual meaning.

The resources of the Church, in short, are limited only by the arts and sciences of man. All the wisdom man has accumulated through centuries of experience, the True Church will regard as holy, and its task it will conceive as the application of specific techniques to human problems. Literature, the fruits of science and industry, all alike are sacred, and that Church alone can hold itself divine which employs to their fullest extent God's revelations to mankind. The religious spirit requires that this world be made the best world possible.

IV

IT IS THE WAY TO THE SECRET SPRING

MILLIONS without and thousands within the contemporary Church have lost the path to the secret spring. The Church's holy resources will give the individual sustenance along his way but only drinking at the secret spring will give him strength to persist in the process of spiritual growth so that he will know progress in the life of the spirit. The path to the spring is prayer and worship. The purpose of the True Church is to lead the seeker and to provide him fellowship, to point out the path and to encourage him to drink.

I

"Prayer is the lost word," says George Buttrick in his book, *Prayer*. It is the lost word, the lost act of man's lost soul. The soul lives only when nourished by the spring eternal. One must thirst, he must go to the spring and, if he is to live, he must drink not once but again and again. He is never fully filled, never receiving enough. For the more he lives, the more he seeks the wonder, the majesty, the glory of life.

What is worship? It is man's response in prayer and praise, in confession and adoration, to God's outflow, to His revealing. Worship is man's response to God as revealed in nature, in the divine in men, in crises of the soul, in Jesus Christ, and in those in every age who have been fired with the divine spark. It is the experience of the soul searching for its counterpart. Worship is the cry of thirsty land for rain; the quest of a brooklet for the ocean. It is the rapture of a poet enthralled by the beauty of a sunrise; the quiet of a workman pausing to listen to a strain of music; the search of a hungry heart for love. It is the engulfing of individual self in the universal self. It is man's ascent of the altar stairs to God and his return to live so that others will climb and live. It is the flow of time into eternity.

Worship is fellowship between the soul and its Maker. Boynton Merrill says:

What is worship? It is commerce between my soul and my soul's Maker. It is a sending forth of the ships of my need and the returning of those ships laden with His strength. It is coming into the presence of something mightier than I am, which at once humbles me and yet makes me long to be stronger than I am. It is coming under the spell of something purer than I am, and by it, being moved to say "I would be a better man than I am." Whatever the thing may be, if it humbles us, if it gives us a vision of duty, if it exalts us, if it sends us back into the busy world with a steadying spell upon us and if, above all, it makes us aware of God, it is worship.

Worship reaches its noblest height probably when men come, deliberately and hopefully, alone or in great companies, into the cleansing, kindling presence of Him whom we call God. When men who believe in God deliberately set apart places and hours that He may have a chance to renew their hearts, to speak their minds, to strengthen their wills, to heal their hurts and to breathe upon their hopes we have worship of a high order.

The aim of true worship is God re-seen and man re-made.

"O world invisible, we view thee,
O world intangible, we touch thee."

Yes, the purpose of worship is the linking and the leaguing of these finite lives of ours with the infinite life and love of God. Worship is, I believe, the first duty and the greatest privilege of the Christian Church for worship is the first and the only ultimate need of man.[1]

Once when a minister went into his sanctuary, he found there a young soldier who asked, "Do you mind if I sit here?"

"Of course not," the minister assured him, "that is why this church is always open."

"Thanks," the soldier added, "I love to come here. It makes you quiet inside and it makes you feel bigger than you are."

"Quiet inside"—the world is stilled for a bit and God is given His chance. Man made "bigger than he is"—because to his own small life has been added something out of the life of Him who first gave us life and who ever seeks to renew and exalt it. Worship is, as Thomas Kelly made so clear in *A Testament of Devotion*, growing from a multitude of selves that outvote one another into one self. And more, it is the way by which the self finds unity with God. In worship, the self no longer centers in itself nor talks to itself. In worship, the individual speaks with God. He thinks the thoughts of God as revealed in Christ and in the prophets and the saints of all ages. He loves what God loves and dreams the dreams of God. He is no longer a figure of earth but a mirror of God. Then God lives in him and reaches others through him.

Worship is inherent in the nature of man. To ask why he worships is to ask why he breathes. When one shuns the spring of God's loving gifts, he betrays his own creation and loses the very purpose of living. When man turns from the path that leads to oneness with God, he blunders into excesses, into futile escapes, into physical and mental maladies and idolatries that end in disillusionment.

[1] A definition of worship submitted to the author by Dr. Boynton Merrill, minister of the First Congregational Church, Columbus, Ohio. Used with his permission.

In the True Church the main emphasis is always on finding the way to the secret spring. It is an emphasis sadly lacking in the contemporary Church. To confirm its absence one has only to count the few—often no more than a handful of members— who share in the morning or evening worship services of their Church. And when an observer senses the lifelessness of the congregations found in many of the local units of the contemporary Church, he cannot help but ask, "Is *this* what the Church is seeking to accomplish? If the Church is lifeless here, if there is no vitality here, where then is there vitality?"

On the part of those who are truly devoted, there is recognition of the need to relight the fire on the altars of the soul of the visible and invisible Church. They know that there is a new tide of hunger for spiritual things and for public worship. The contemporary Church either stresses the intellectual and emphasizes human resources, forgetting that the human mind, great as it is, is not enough; or it plays up a type of emotionalism that cannot issue into God-guided conduct. Frank Laubach feels that a far-flung revival of spiritual awakening is ready to dawn if the Church can lead it. That will only be possible with the rediscovery of the path that leads to the secret spring, with the resurrender of human will to the Divine, and with the rebirth of life eternal in the soul of man.

If public worship vanishes, the Church and the Christian ethic will die with it. Robert J. McCracken, in one of his first sermons in Riverside Church, said this:

The Church has other things to do but if it is to do them and to do them well, it must live and its life depends on its worship. Let it neglect or abandon that and it has lost its integrating principle, the source and secret of its vitality and power. The Quakers have a magnificent record in the field of social service but how long would they survive as a Christian body if they gave up their "Meetings for Worship"? Those meetings constitute the center and core of the whole movement. As with the Quakers, so with all true church-men and so with you here. This Church which cost so much to build and which it costs so much to maintain, was reared for the public worship of God. This service is the diamond pivot around which all the agencies of the congregation revolve. And why? Because you realize that practical urgencies must never be permitted to blind you to the eternal verities. You serve God and your fellows but you are careful to put the service of God first. That is something we dare not let drop! Always we must set ourselves to survey the contemporary scene from the viewpoint of eternity and work out here what we have seen there. The "heavenly vision" must be the most formative influence we know, giving to our minds perspective, to our characters stability, to our activities direction and inspiration.[2]

Before all else, the Christian community is a fellowship united by worship of the God and Father of us all. That is the essential bond of unity, the condition on which co-operation rests. It lies deep in the hearts of all those who have found the secret of the spiritual life. It is primary in the hearts of those who are committed to the fact that we are spiritual and that the purpose of our lives is to develop that spiritual nature. If the members of the contemporary Church do not share together the central and primary religious experience, they will not remain a Church at all.

The solution does not lie in a barren and negative approach. The lost path to the secret spring will not be rediscovered by pleas and entreaties to the young, or by presenting it as a painful Christian duty, or still less by devising artful attractions to lure youth inside the sanctuary. The True Church faces the whole matter of finding this lost path in a more fundamental way.

[2] *Current Religious Thought*, Vol. VI, 1946, p. 1.

We have already pointed out, in the first chapter, that many people have ceased to hope that the Church can satisfy their instinctive need for worship. They must either allow the instinct to wither or to seek satisfaction in the activities of our sensate culture. Many of these activities take them out of themselves, but they never take them to God. The True Church can only win their leadership by regaining the capacity for worship. That this cannot be accomplished by a few simple revisions of program is apparent. It can only be done through an acceptance of acknowledged creative principles and a clear apprehension as to what, as worshipers, we are asking for and what we expect to receive. The True Church needs solid theological background and power of imaginative interpretation. In the next chapter we shall speak of some of the ventures of the True Church, one of which is theological. Dr. Alfred North Whitehead has said:

The defect of the liberal theology of the last two hundred years is that it has confined itself to the suggestion of minor valid reasons why people should continue to go to Church in the traditional fashion.[3]

To the True Church this is the crux of the whole situation. A sound and vital theology is necessary, but the allegiance of the new age to the Divine will only be won through true worship.

Worship begins, as it ends, in wonder. In essence, it is the outreach of man to the spiritual presence in his environment. In it alone is his life fulfilled. To worship is to take the path to the secret spring, where God meets the soul of man. Worship is an innate desire. Even at the most primitive level, where it may not amount to more than a dim recognition of the supernatural, it has, nevertheless, had a coercive quality. The object of worship is always regarded as exercising a claim on the worshiper, and

[3] *Adventures of Ideas*, by Alfred North Whitehead (New York: The Macmillan Company, 1933), p. 208.

therefore is sacred rather than merely awed. Thus worship starts, not in any activities which we originate but in those which God brings to bear upon us. Just as, in the order of nature, all growth and all advance in knowledge are by way of response to environment, so it is that in the realm of the spirit we grow in grace and in understanding by way of response to God. As we have said, what we call the offering of worship is our response to that touch of God in our hearts and minds which is grace. Worship and grace are related as action and contemplation are related. It is God who invokes the response which He rewards. Worship is man's many and varied responses to the claim of God upon him. When man responds to God's revealing, when he takes the path to the secret spring, his own soul finds fulfillment of its nature in personal communion with God. His own soul becomes alive with the life that is the nature of God.

Worship in its deepest meaning is the hallowing of God's name. This is the end for which man was created, to glorify God and enjoy Him forever, to glorify all His creation. The worshiper responds in the fullest sense to the claims and gifts and tasks which God presents to him. The worshiper is redeemed from blindness, from listlessness, from self-concern, and is liberated into new insight and richer service for the glory of God. Christian worship finds its fulfillment when the worshiper is admitted to communion with God's redemptive activity in the world. God is glorified when His sons "finish the work He has given them to do." The worship of the Church fails if it does not succeed in relating the response of the worshipers to God's other claims in the broad field of life as a whole and in associating the wide, rich interests of human life with an acceptance of His will for each generation.

There are fruits of worship which must come into being if we are to solve even the simplest problems that haunt us in this new age. Worship has great values for us—it gives us renewed life and power; it cleanses and strengthens us, discloses God to us. Worship takes our eyes from self and lifts them to God and omnipotence. Only when we kneel before that which is greater can we be stronger. Worship, while it humbles, also exalts. Dr. Albert W. Palmer, of Chicago, relates how Lorado Taft spent hours experimenting with lighting. He found inspiration in seeing how a piece of sculpture could change under the influence of light and shadow. One day Dr. Palmer saw him at work on Donatello's statue, "The Boy St. John." Lighted from below, the face of the statue held the empty look of a moron, but when lighted from above, it showed the radiant glance of an angel. There is a commentary that hits straight at the heart of the problem. Is not one of our troubles due to the fact that lighting of human life comes from below? From cheap movies, cheap literature, cheap talk—from the whole sordid array of cheap appeals that surrounds us. But in worship the light shines from above, bathing the kneeling figure of the worshiper in radiance.

Worship gives faith and confidence. Why do we shrink from it? Why do we deny ourselves its support? "They that wait upon the Lord shall renew their strength; they shall mount up with wings as eagles; they shall run, and not be weary. . . ." And, if we worship God, we know that nothing "neither death, nor life, nor angels, nor principalities, nor powers, nor things present, nor things to come, nor height, nor depth, nor any other creature, shall be able to separate us from the love of God, which is in Christ Jesus our Lord."

Worship sharpens our purpose and keeps it vivid within us.

It gives us the power to go on. Through it we get the stuff to save us from losing heart.

II

To understand the tasks before the True Church in helping individuals rediscover this lost path of prayer and worship to the secret spring of Life Eternal, there are several states of mind in the modern world that need illumination.

There is an emotional aloneness, a homesickness of soul, that is widespread today. It springs from many sources. It is due, in part, to the movement of peoples from one place to another. In part, it is the result of a world in terrible plight—a world in which millions can merely exist, millions of children are orphaned of their parents, fathers and mothers are separated, many husbands have been killed. But the more fundamental cause of this emotional aloneness is the vastness of the universe. There is a homeless quality created by the very bigness of things. Only worship can help human beings overcome the tendency to cower before the vastness of nature, can save them from cringing before its bigness and from being slaves of its size. Only in worship can the soul find the capacity to assert its own validity. Only when the soul enters into God and becomes alive with God does it find that significance.

As far as we know, in all the realm of nature of which man is a part, he is the only being aware of himself. He alone can contemplate the nature from which he comes, rejoice in its beauty, stand in awe before its majesty, and shrink from its terrors. And perhaps that day of self-awareness in man is a day both of triumph and tragedy. The mountain does not recognize itself as a mountain and signal to the river that winds about its base in its determined progress to the sea. The high hills never break into song. The wide sea knows not the joy and grief of the lover nor the lonely loyalty of the martyr. The star-strewn sky, vast and bewildering, cannot feel its own mystery and majesty. "Though the universe encompass me," exclaimed Pascal, "by thought I encompass the universe." He meant that the vast realm of nature is not cognizant of itself but that you and I, so insignificant in size and strength, are aware of ourselves and of the universe. And ponder this—all meanings are read into nature by man; the universe does not endow itself with value. Markings in ink upon paper are not a poem unless man touches it into immortality. A political event, a scientific concept, have no meaning except that which man gives to them. Men enrich life with meanings that endure long after they are gone. We still think Socrates' thoughts after him; Shakespeare has long slept in his Avon tomb, but the world yet widens under his vision.

In Frederick Myers' essay on Vergil[4] he shows how many individual lines of *The Aeneid* have gone into the making of world history. Enumerating each, he tells its story:

On this line the poet's own face faltered as he read; here is the verse which Augustine quotes as typical of all the pathos and glory of pagan art from which Christians must flee; this is the couplet which saintly Fenelon could never read without admiring tears; this is the line Filippo Strazzi scrawled upon his prison wall before he took his life to avoid worse ill. These are the lines like a trumpet call which roused Savonarola to seek the things above, and this is the line Dante heard in the "Paradise of God." But does the universe preserve the works and destroy the worker: Can it be that the song is greater than the singer and the thoughts more enduring than the thinker? This strange being, man—so frail, so mighty, a part of nature but alone aware of himself and nature; he who alone

[4] Quoted in *The Human Situation*, by William Macneile Dixon (New York: Longman, Green and Company, 1937).

finds meanings and creates them—in a universe that conserves its energies, shall he alone be destroyed? Nay, rather in whatever altered garments, the mind shall survive "While castles fade and empires fall asleep."

It is only in worship that the soul, as it meets God, becomes alive with eternal life for any given moment. Then, in that isolated moment, the individual is at home in his universe. He is no longer a cosmic orphan, but a part of the Divine Presence.

Knowing this union with God, having this awareness of God, by no means leads the individual to complacency. Rather, it makes him yearn to follow the path and to come to the spring over and over again, eager to lead others there, eager to drink with them. It makes him sensitive to visions of truth that will never let him go. It frees him to respond to those nameless longings that ever lure him onward.

The deepest satisfactions of life beget the deepest longings. When we look upon the "Sistine Madonna," or hear Beethoven's *Ninth Symphony*, or see an unspeakably beautiful sunset, or feel the impact of a God-filled life, it gives us joy and peace. But it awakens, too, infinite yearnings that call us above and beyond the bondage of selfish desires. The tenderest human love with its kindly comradeship is a haven in which the ships of desire find rest, but it is also a harbor from which they set sail for the calling deeps. A philosopher once walked by the seaside with a young woman and listened to her talk of love and its beauty. Suddenly she stooped to pick up a pebble and showed it to him, glinting white and green and gold. As they walked on, she told of her faith in love and its power to fulfill life completely. But the philosopher said, "Show me the pebble again, the one your hand holds so tightly." She reached out her hand and revealed it, not shining and beautiful but dull and dry.

"There," he said, "you see, you must not pick up pretty pebbles if you do not want them to lose their luster; you must leave them where the waves of the ocean can roll over them." Going back, the young woman replaced her pebble upon the beach. Her face was not happy until she had seen the waves break over it, bathe it, and then recede. These human loves of ours, our deep satisfactions—they give us greatest joy and show their richest colors when they are overswept by the mysterious tides of an infinite sea.

The longing of love that comes so sharply in the gray day of bereavement is always present within us. The truest love is the merging of the infinite longing of two human souls. It is not the cure of the soul's loneliness. It is comradeship in loneliness. Suffering and longing and agony are at the core of all human experience; the spirit of man confesses itself a stranger upon the earth. Indeed, when man is no longer disquieted, when he no more feels within himself the restlessness of one athirst, he has ceased to be human and his soul has become a desert. It is the lost soul that feels no pangs of great desire, nor any hurt of noble discontent.

We may achieve a degree of success in making earth our home and sense our satisfaction, but it is difficult to do. For, by its very nature, life is not a destination, but a journey; not an ending, but a beginning. It is hard to interpret it rationally in any other way. Not that we should undervalue the earthly life, its joys and achievements—that is not the point. There was a time when religion did disparage it overmuch. But Michelangelo would not agree that his sculpture was no more than a pleasant pastime, nor Raphael that his canvases were only the aimless expression of an artistic dilettante. Keats with his poetry, Darwin with his biologic postulates, Einstein with the theory of relativity—none of these would admit that the substance of his work has no greater value than the sum of his earthly years. And they are right, for truth and beauty have a value and significance of their own without reference to time or place. Some might say that devotion to beauty and truth and goodness is, in itself, an attempt to reach out and grasp for man a brief hold on the Eternal. Certainly the highest art and the most patient search for truth has behind it the sense of a pilgrimage. Who would ever conceive of gaining so much knowledge and wisdom that he could ultimately sit by the fireside and say, "Now I have garnered all the truth." Who has ever thought of an immortal canvas or of a deathless poem save as a small gleam of perfect beauty, caught by a winged soul and molded in concrete form? The greatest art has been produced by pilgrims on their journey in quest of eternal beauty. There is a lyric in which George Herbert describes how, when God first made man, He poured out upon him all the blessings he could contain—love, strength, beauty, wisdom, honor and pleasure. Just one He withheld. And that was rest, the blessing of peace. Herbert said of these gifts:

> Yet let him keep the rest
> But keep them with repining restlessness;
> Let him be weak and weary, that at last,
> If goodness lead him not, then weariness
> May turn him to my breast.

Adelaide Proctor speaks of "Joy, tender and true, yet all with wings, so earth's bliss may be our guide but not our chain." That is the view of the healthy soul, and a view true to the soul's deep necessities.

Life is a maze of beginnings without endings. Completions

seem forever withheld. What lover feels that he has exhausted love? What poet feels that he has put into song the final wordless wonder of his soul? What saint felt that he had done more than to take a few faltering steps up the high paths of Christly living? Here again life is true to the necessities of the soul, for we live only as we reach forward. The most subtle temptation that can try the soul comes with high achievement and deep insight, such as that which came to Faust when he said, "Let me hold this moment of attainment and stop here satisfied." We must pursue goals destined ever to elude us. We must seek values that forever cry, "There are more and better ahead." All other ends wither the soul.

William Ernest Hocking argues:

The incompleteness of our attainment may defeat the more superficial and dated self but is true to the deepest self within us. It is the destiny of the dated self not to be completed at any moment —that half-painted picture, that unfinished symphony, that partly-plowed field, that deserted campaign, that almost-grasped idea. These are the broken edges of history left forever as futurist images of action going on—and insofar truer to the living self than the repose of a partly concluded task[5]

These words recall the motto of St. Catharine, "Care not to present a finished work to God who is infinite in love and demands of thee only infinite desire." It was Browning's Grammarian, realizing there was so much to be and to do that he never attained, who said, "But man has forever." We must give up our lust of finishing. If we finish our tasks, they will be too small; if we set for ourselves goals which we can reach, they will prove not worth the reaching.

[5] From *Thoughts on Death and Life*, by William Ernest Hocking (New York: Harper & Brothers, 1937), p. 29.

If life has no higher destiny than to live a few years snatched out of eternity, then the best of it is a mockery. Then we are here to build ships that shall never sail the sea; to lay a foundation upon which shall rise no cathedral groin or agonizing spire. Then we are here to love and lose, and all our deepest longings are but an echo of the laughter of a careless universe. But there is a better view. The continual craving for that which is not, the persistent anxiety and pain which lie at the core of being, the deep-buried concern which the pessimist interprets as the defeat of our happiness—those, in reality, make up the soul's loyalty to its own goal, its underlying faithfulness to its destiny. So Paul looked at life: "I count not myself to have apprehended: but this one thing I do, forgetting those things which are behind, and reaching forth unto those things which are before, I press toward the mark for the prize of the high calling of God in Christ Jesus."

As one finds the path to the spring of life eternal, traveling it alone and in fellowship with others who share his thirst and longing, he finds union with God in himself and with them, and he begins to know the eternal life that is the very heart of the universe. He is at home in time and beyond time, and the longings that haunt him and the recurring thirst that compels him will have meaning. Finding the spring that makes his soul a garden in which grow the fruits of God's love, righteousness and mercy, he will reveal the path to others.

> I go to prove my soul:
> I see my way as birds their trackless way—
> I shall arrive: what time, what cometh first
> I ask not: but unless God send His hail
>   or blinding fireballs, sleet, or stifling snow,
> In some time—His good time—I shall arrive.
>   He guides me and the bird.

III

There are other reasons why the path is lost. There are count-less influences playing upon the individual today which make him conscious only of mechanisms and aware only of the visible. These influences make contemplation on the life of the spirit seem foreign. While most people today have some interest in religion, they lack patience and sincere desire for enlightening in sufficient degree to make the necessary sacrifices. They prefer quick results. It was Job who cried, "O, that I knew where I might find Him." And Isaiah said, "Verily, thou are a God that hidest Thyself." In our noisy, blatant age, there remains no reticence but God's. He alone does not thrust Himself upon us. His least intent would be to rob us of the grace of giving, of the discipline of seeking, of the experience of co-creating. He does not lift up his soul and cry on the streets. One does not become aware of the Divine Giver without the combined efforts of mind and heart. A traveler walking under blossom-laden trees along leafy roads may be aware of their beauty without thought of the God who made them. God's signature never graces His gifts. If only, like the artist, He would put His name at the foot of some masterpiece of coloring in the sky; or, like the musician, have His name announced prior to the song of the lark! When God came in full incarnation, it was as a babe in the family of a working man. He trod the hills of His native country and had no place to lay His head.

God is here. He is all about us. The relentless eagerness that drives the scientist in endless research is God. The patience that bears life's overwhelming disasters bravely is God. God is life in the soul and yearning in the heart of the seeker. God is indigna-tion in the soul of man as he weeps over life's injustices and renews himself constantly at the higher spring to build a better world. God is the vision of the seer who looks beyond to behold "alabaster cities . . . undimmed by human tears."

Though God ever seeks men, He is only found by those who diligently seek Him. There is no need to prove the unobtrusiveness of God. He seems hidden when people most need Him. The torch of human knowledge has thus far but lightened the fringes of the night. The search for truth is not a matter for academic study but is bound up in the burden and tragedy and bafflement of living. But we must remember that some of the seeming hiddenness of God is our blindness and not His withdrawing. We are steeped in things, in visibles and tangibles. We build houses rather than homes. We nourish our bodies but deny our souls. We are the victims of bigness. God is in the small, spiritual influences, not in the obtrusive forces of life. God comes like the sighing of the west wind, gentle, mysterious, and soon seeming to be gone.

We do not hear the trailing of God's garments because He passes us in scenes of life's most familiar fashioning. "I never saw God," says one, "I know little of Him. But that which I love most is the unfolding mystery of a child's soul as I behold it in my own home and that which moves me most is the sight of my own child coming down the street to meet me at eventide, crying so joyously, 'Father, father.'" But he has never seen God! "I have never heard the footsteps of God," says another, "but I love the gentle green of spring's first foliage, the soft beauty of meadows and woodland nooks, and the strange way of the fleecy clouds drifting across the tender sky of a May morning." Says another, "Across the street from us I saw two hearts broken and bereft. But, rising from the desolation of their sorrow, I saw them confront life with brave and willing hearts, deepened and sweetened by the Calvary through which they had passed." Yet

they never saw God! No wonder a sensitive heart, knowing our
human blindness, prayed:

> I ask no dream, no prophet ecstasies,
> No sudden rending of the veil of clay,
> No angel visitant, no opening skies;
> But take the dimness of my soul away.

We do have some gleams of the reasons why God does not
intrude Himself, why He seems half-hidden. God leads us on
to the highest exercise of the spirit—complete trust in Him. He
gives us enough glimpses of His creative working and His
loving providence to keep the keen soul alert to the deeper communion and the higher knowledge. In this quest is the noblest
activity of man's soul. It involves his deepest dedication to all
the highest visions that have wooed his spirit and to the finest
causes that have challenged his loyalty. No one ever trusts God
who does not trust Him alike in darkness and in light. He who
can cry, "Thou slayest me, yet will I trust thee," and who, from
a cross can speak that infinitely tender word, "Father"—he has
made life's bravest and most beautiful adventure. God requires
that kind of faith. Without it He is never really known.

We need the risk, the peril. There is a moral ministry in un-
certainty. After Job uttered his poignant cry, "Oh, that I knew
where I might find Him," he spoke of something else, something that God seeks to achieve in our souls while we live in this
world: "But he knoweth the way that I take: when he hath
tried me, I shall come forth as gold. He will bring each one
forth—each one of the distraught and burdened heart, of the
lonely love, of the anxious mind. He knows the way each one
takes and He will bring him forth."

It is for our sakes that the God who reveals Himself also

remains hidden. "It is the glory of God to conceal a thing." Man needs the kind of world that demands that he make it better. Man needs a God who must be sought and trusted. We pluck a fragile flower and, studying its delicate loveliness, we marvel that so frail and beautiful a thing should have fought its way to perfection in spite of frost and rain and storm. But we are wrong to marvel, for all its environment—including the winter winds and beating rain—has helped to make it. The flower has absorbed from the best of its environment, has struggled with the worst of it, and has won from all of it its magical beauty and fragrance. Summer sunshine alone cannot explain a flower. It needs winter nights and frozen earth and harsh winds. So man is made—is being made—by the whole of his environment, including the mystery and the tragedy of life and the seeming withdrawal of God.

God has shown His moral beauty and life's everlasting meaning in Him who said, "He that hath seen me hath seen the Father." We need not lose the way even though at times we seem to tread it alone. When the way lies through darkness, when its guideposts and lights seem to have failed us, then we must look into the face of Jesus so that He may command and strengthen and comfort us. Is the world dark? He is the light that lighteth every man who cometh into the world. Behold, He stands at the gate to the path and leads us to the spring.

IV

What makes worship a transforming experience? There are two experiences in the Old Testament that throw light on the question. Moses turned aside as he heard God's voice. He took a path from the main road. Worshipers, too, must turn aside; they must give God a chance. Moses covered his face, humbled and shaken by his experience. But God spoke to his heart and changed him and charged him with a task: "Set my people free." And when Moses, fearful, asked, "Who am I that I should go?" God answered, "Behold, I will be with thee." Moses went. God kept His word. The frightened keeper of the herd became one of the world's greatest leaders and lawmakers.

To recall the experience of Isaiah is to the point. He saw "the Lord sitting upon a throne, high and lifted up." The experience humbled him. "Woe is me," he cried. "I am a man of unclean lips, and I dwell in the midst of a people of unclean lips." Redeemed from unworthiness, he caught a vision of a task to be done, saying, "Here am I; send me." Isaiah became one of Israel's greatest prophets.

The transforming effect of corporate worship follows such a pattern. There is a vision of God, a humbling and lifting up of the soul. Disclosure and acceptance of a task follow, and finally, assurance and experience of God's sustaining presence. These are the stages in worship.

In the True Church, the minister does not worship or pray or think for the worshipers, but with them. Together they listen for the still, small voice. Together they confess their human weaknesses and seek the healing, life-giving waters of the eternal spring. The channels of the soul are cleared, so that the life of God may flow through them.

What are some of the moods conceived in worship? They are not moods created by men but moods impressed by the Divine deep into the consciousness of those who have traveled the path and found the presence of God. If a service is to be genuine and life-giving, it leads the worshiper to wait in the presence of the eternal God gladly and quietly and expectantly. It helps the worshiper to remember his own human frailty and to face honestly the fact that he has not always been strong. It brings to him vividly and overwhelmingly a sense of the divine love that forever seeks him out and will not let him go. The Church helps the worshiper to glimpse God's holy purpose and God's need of His children, and then sends him out to live in and through God among men.

The service itself has an unhurried tempo. It breathes the spirit of divine life. It moves easily and is peace-producing. It centers itself in the heart of each worshiper, uniting and leading them to a centeredness in God. It begins with people as they are, leading them to the spring where they meet God and surrender fully to Him. There is spirit and vitality in the service. The minister, the choir, and others who lead in the service are alive with the very life and radiance of God within them. There is warmth and fellowship in the bearing of the ushers and all others who serve as guides along the pathway of worship. What are the elements of the service? As the worshipers gather they soon come to know the redeeming power of silence. The organ prelude cleanses, leading them out of the rush and hurry of life, to listen for the Master's voice in quietness. Emerson said, "I like the quiet Church." And Boynton Merrill remembers that "night and dawn and spring come in quietness; so, too, does the quickening of the spirit."

The processional hymn carries with it something of the greatness, the wonder and glory, the power of God. "A Mighty Fortress is Our God"—"Come Thou Almighty King"—"I Saw the Lord High and Lifted Up"—"He Is the Lord God Omnipotent Who Reigneth"—"The Heavens Declare the Glory of God and the Firmament Showeth His Handiwork"—"He is the God Who Guides the Stars in Their Courses and Healeth the Broken and the Contrite Heart." The processional hymn leads the worshiper into His presence and creates awareness of His omnipotence and His power. "Holy, Holy, Holy, Lord God Almighty"—that is the first attitude, that is the first mood, that is the mighty consensus of feeling that marks the first stage in worship.

Following the processional hymn is the call to worship. It is the pronouncement of blessed words that have come down out of the past, words of consecrated saints and prophets who in the past have spoken to the Almighty and received His answer. In the call to worship, the worshiper listens and responds, using their words, catching something of their high experiences, and sensing their experiences as his own. The worshiper identifies himself with them, becomes articulate in their words. "Who shall ascend into the hill of the Lord? or who shall stand in his holy place? He that hath clean hands, and a pure heart; who hath not lifted up his soul unto vanity, nor sworn deceitfully. He shall receive the blessing from the Lord, and righteousness from the God of his salvation."

It is in the call to worship that the worshiper is led to a realization of his own mortality. As he contemplates the Eternal One, he finds eternity in his own years. While the worshiper is finite, God is infinite. While he is weak, God is infinitely strong. Aware of his weakness, the worshiper comes to rejoice in the strength of Jehovah. Admitting his shortcomings, he gives utterance to the hope of becoming better. The worshiper does not grovel, he is not worthless clay nor miserable sinner in whom there is no health. There is health in him because God is within him, because he is a child of God. But, like a child, he may fail. When his soul's health is touched with sickness, it is the Lord that created him in the beginning who makes him whole. The searcher may have done well during the foregoing week, he may have been unselfish and may consciously have hurt no one. In such an instance, his confession will not be weighed down with regret but will still be spurred with the need of doing better. If, during the foregoing week, one has achieved a degree of harmony with the will of God, he is more than ever aware that about him is the debris of a shattered, broken world. Everywhere about him is the evidence that he lives in the midst of a people who have fallen short of the glory of God, with whom he shares the common guilt for the sins of the world.

In the experience of true worship, the individual senses his common guilt for the catastrophe which twice has fallen upon the world—world war, with its hideous aftermath of hunger and famine and world-wide estrangement of man from his brother. In worship he becomes aware of the truth that this generation must live by the will of God or perish.

To the service of worship the individual brings his confession. Reminded that the good which good people fail to do is more significant than the evil which bad men do, he seeks forgiveness for sins of omission and commission. He searches his heart, on guard lest he stand aloof, thanking God that he is not as other men.

Thus, in the call to worship, there is recognition of the goodness and the power and the glory of God. The searcher sees his own weakness and becomes aflame with hope of growing in the will of God, with assurance of forgiveness and of pardon and of God's presence and life. It is followed by the Lord's Prayer, which is the perfect prayer, and by an anthem that confirms these high moods, that keeps the soul and the heart and mind in tune with the Divine Presence.

This is the first stage in worship, the first step along the path to the spring. The service is marked by an awareness of the omnipotence, wonder and glory of God, by a realization of human need. Its vital values are the individual's consciousness of God's goodness and his outflow of gratitude to God.

Then comes to the worshiper the voice of God through the scripture. It must be well chosen and its reading effective. In some units of the Church, young people and lay members are asked to read the scripture, which provides participation and gives the congregation a sense of representation. The reading of the scripture should be done with the spirit of love and reality. After the words of God through the scripture and other holy writings, there follow the words of the congregation to God. In one unit of the Church this is a period of responsive reading between congregation and choir: "O Lord, show thy mercy upon us." And the choir sings: "And grant us Thy salvation." The people respond, "O God, make clean our hearts within us," and the choir, "And take not Thy holy spirit from us." Complete silence follows, for group meditation and group waiting.

The pastoral prayer is in simple words from the minister's heart. The pastor does not pray too long, remembering that the attention span of the average person is not great. The minister should take into account four emphases in the morning prayer: First, gratitude and thankfulness; second, confession; third, commitment; and finally, intercession for the Church universal, for the leaders of the nations of the earth and for those still so rooted to the earth that they live without conscious thought of God.

One very important point in constructing the pastoral prayer is to avoid putting the burden of service and activity and problem-solving on God. The petition of a prayer asking God to take care of the hungry and the "unsaved," and to bless the missionaries is not psychologically good. A prayer should be so worded as to present the worshiper as a co-operator with God. Instead of asking God to feed the hungry, the petition on the other hand might be worded thus: "O God, use us to help Thee feed the hungry. Help us to release those who are now not free so that they may grow in a knowledge of Thee and find the path they have lost, or never known, to the secret spring. O God, use us to help illumine and support our leaders in every aspect of our collective will." Prayer is only vital when it leads to co-operation with God. Prayer and work are equally expressions of the religious spirit.

The offering is important in the service with a purpose far more significant than that of obtaining money. For those who have become aware of the goodness and glory of God, who have sensed their need of God and have met God and become alive at the spring, it is an opportunity to make some visible sign of their gratitude. It is an opportunity to practice their stewardship. Having freely received, they freely give. Loving God, they give testimony by sharing that with which God has blessed them.

The sermon is another way for God to speak, through the mind and heart of the minister, to those who worship. It most often uses the spoken word, but may conceivably use picture or drama. But whatever the media of the sermon's presentation, it is a way by which God may speak to worshipers in the beloved fellowship of the sanctuary. While the sermon is over-emphasized in the contemporary Church, so that people often come to worship the minister rather than God, it does have a very important and fundamental place in the fellowship of the way to the spring. In another chapter we will discuss the new preaching that the new Church demands.

What is the climax of a genuine service of worship? It must

be stated clearly: The goal of every sermon and the goal of worship itself is the dedication of self to God by those who have united in the great experience of waiting together in His house and in His presence. Following the sermon there must be a period of silence for self-dedication, for marshaling of the will, and for surrendering the mind to the high and holy will of God. Having shared with Christ, the worshipers go forth to walk in His steps. Having met God in the sanctuary of the soul, they go forth to live His will and reveal His life, so that others will seek Him and will find the path and follow it to the living spring.

Then the benediction to remind the worshiper again of God's power, of His peace and love, and of His constant present. These are the steps along the path to the spring, the stages of worship in the True Church: to see the Lord, "high and lifted up"; to come to know Him, to hear Him ask, "Who will go?"; to accept His commitment, "Send us"; and, finally, to receive His assurance, "And, lo, I am with you alway, even unto the end of the world."

The spirit of the ushers, to mention an incidental item, is important to their manner of greeting people. The degree to which they love the Church and know God, and the extent to which the life of God and the awareness of God are within them, are reflected in their approach to others. The dedication and spirit of the choir are significant. Choir members, like the minister, are leaders in worship. The organist and the minister of music are as vital to the service as the minister. All work together in true unity to develop a thematic service of worship.

It is very important that the worshipers be acquainted with the hymns of the Church and it is vital that they come to a realization of the place of poetry and music in worship. The contemporary Church has failed to make this clear, so that hymns and sacred music have lost their significance and meaning. While alone they are no guarantee of worship, they are a great aid and are conducive to achieving the moods of worship.

Poetry is the natural language of religion, because religion is experience on a plane that logic cannot reach. The deepest truths of religion are most often apprehended through the approach of the artist. Much of the barrenness and not a few of the misunderstandings that divide the Christian Church are the result of thinking of religion as a science. We have made religion the source of definitions rather than the inspiration of dreams. We have sought its truths by reason rather than by imagination. Had Jesus used our terminology, where he used the word "faith" he might have said "imagination." So much of his vital truth comes to us through images.

Religion has its religious scaffolding, and it ought to be as firmly built and as carefully secured as possible. Religion is realization and spiritual awareness. One finds its meaning as he learns to know the beauty of a landscape, the power of a poem, the soul of a friend, the inspiration of love and surrender. He who is confronted by physical force must overcome it, but he who knows spiritual force must consent to be mastered by it. That is equally true whether one seeks the holiness of beauty in art or whether he seeks the beauty of holiness in religion and worship. The seeker must yield the sovereignty of his spirit until worship shall control the courses of his soul.

For the inexpressible to find expression, it needs the measures of poetry. That is why religion's deepest truths cannot be argued, but must be sung. How lifting are these lines: "The Lord is my shepherd; I shall not want. He maketh me to lie down in green pastures. He leadeth me beside the still waters.

He restoreth my soul: he leadeth me in the paths of righteous-ness for his name's sake. . . ." Or these: "I will lift up mine eyes unto the hills, from whence cometh my help. My help cometh from the Lord, which made heaven and earth. . . ."

In the contemporary Church, creed is so often an attempt, for the purpose of intellectual understanding and agreement, to shut up within the limits of a definition the soul's experience of God. It is natural that these deep and varied experiences of the soul should overflow all vessels made to contain them. That is why poetry, psalms, hymns, oratorios and anthems are the handmaiden of religion because they seek not to restrain thought but to release it. Poetry does not seek to hide the rest-less road within a villa, and to confine it behind geranium bor-ders and palings. The poetry of our great hymns and oratorios seeks ever to push back horizons and to bid men behold the stars. The power of poetry is not in definition but in sugges-tion. Its aim is not to mark plainly and to map, but to beget the haunting lure of distant hills. So the language of religion, even when it defines, never seeks to confine, for religion is made of convictions, of hopes, of aspirations, of loves that well and surge in the soul from some "mystic ocean whose rim no foot has trod." It does not follow, therefore, that religion is unreal. Rather, it is so real that its meaning cannot be contained within the limits of language. And so poetry, with its wist and woe, its rich suggestion and its hint of ever-calling hills, is one of the best modes of expressing that which can never be wholly im-prisoned either in syllogism or in song.

In the True Church use will be made of great music, poetry and oratory, now a part of our spiritual heritage. Each unit of the True Church has a number of choirs for little children, young people and men and women. It has glee clubs of girls and women, of boys and men. These consecrated groups bring the message of the Divine. The great poets, saints and singers of the ages, in communion with the Infinite One, recorded their experience in anthem and hymn, in song and poem. Through them the worshiper gets a vision of the meeting of a vital soul with the very soul of God. Through them he himself is fed, set free, made new.

Thus do the choirs and glee clubs add to the experience of worship. Children, young people and men and women must be taught great hymns and the stories of their background. They must become acquainted with great oratorios and anthems. Singing of the hymns is a source of participation as well as of instruction. Children should be taught to memorize great psalms and great hymns. When a group of worshipers join together they can come with one song and with one gladness in participation. Together they find something that no one person can ever find alone. There the beloved community is born.

In the True Church there are many services of worship. Each unit of the True Church, if large enough, with a sufficient variety of leadership and adequate equipment, has two or three or more services of worship in the morning. In the afternoon there often is a vesper service in which the emphasis is on bringing the message of God through anthem and oratorio, through poetry and song. Someone has well said, "Tell me the songs a people sing and I will tell you what they believe."

While within each unit of the Church there is the corporate experience of worship, as has been described, the True Church seeks to provide a variety of additional experiences of worship in all departments of the children's church school. There is training in worship and in the experiences of worship, and in the appreciation and use of the materials of worship. The same plan holds for the youth groups. In one unit of the Church, the various youth groups come together in the sanctuary in the evening for preparing and sharing in creative experiences of worship. In these groups there are varying emphases, and varying use is made of light and color, the voice, drama and music. The values obtained in planning such experiences may be equal to those of the actual experience of worship.

The True Church looks upon the summer camp as a great opportunity not only for training young people in worship but for helping them find a reality in worship out-of-doors which is not possible within a building. Here there is the resource of the natural world. Here worship may be less formal than in the sanctuary, but emphasis is laid on the same great stages and moods in the path to the secret spring.

In units of the True Church there would be prayer cells—small groups that gather for prayer and meditation. One unit might have a group of young people meeting Thursday night at 5:30 when they gather in the sanctuary for a half hour's silent meditation. Afterward, they sit around a table, in the spirit of Jesus and his disciples in the upper room. There they share together their common quest for the life of the spirit, guided by the values made available in the Bible and by the insights of saints through all the ages.

Groups of this sort are growing in a number of local churches. It is the consensus of judgment that such a group should include not more than fifteen persons. Some churches are developing a number of these groups and are finding them to be a sacred nucleus within the body of the Church from which comes power and from which a new spirit is transfused into the very blood stream of the church family. One parish has a communion service each Sunday morning. After a time of preparation, individuals come into the chancel and kneel, each seeking his own quiet and personal experience with God.

V

There are three tests of the efficacy of corporate worship in the True Church. First, it leads into private prayer and worship so that the individual becomes increasingly centered in God and lives by His continual guidance. It also leads into the creation of small cells for worship and growth in the life of the spirit. Second, the insights of worship are woven into all areas of living. The worshiper so lives that others will worship God, growing in their faith and their knowledge of Him and in hunger for His will. Being forgiven, they learn to forgive. Receiving mercy, they are merciful. Centered in the goodness of God, they are gracious. Alive with the love that is God, they live by love, kindness and gentleness. Being at home with God, they know the faith that banishes fear, the love that forbids resentment and hate.

The third test rests on the fact that the hour of corporate worship in the True Church is the focusing of a large variety of reciprocal ministries, ventures in truth-seeking, in problem-solving, and in training in all aspects of building the beloved community. Those who worship will find the experience more meaningful if they not only know one another, but if they come to the service as comrades in other activities as well. Worship in its fullest sense means individual and group union with God, together with a common realization of the life that is eternal.

One Sunday morning a man went to worship in a sanctuary where he had never been before. He was astonished. Though a stranger, he immediately became aware that here was a beloved fellowship. There were warmth and love abounding, not only between members of the congregation but for him. The approach of the usher warmed his heart—it was too sponta- neous to be other than real. He said to himself, "This is like my own home. It is good to be here!" He became relaxed and thoughtful. Soon the feeling grew upon him that this was holy ground. He became aware of God, the great and wonderful, the all-powerful and infinite, yet the protector of each child; of God, the guider of the stars and healer of the lonely heart; of God, the Father of all men and his own father. He looked about him, marveling at the quiet radiance in the faces of the worshipers. Kinship grew in his heart. Then and there he found the home of his soul. He worshiped. Filled by the waters of the spring, he felt cleansed and empowered to go forth into the coming week.

Following the benediction many greeted him in love and thoughtfulness. There were no inquiries whether he belonged there; only a few asked him his name. He met and talked with one of the leading laymen of the Church, speaking of his own transforming experience. "I have never known such warmth and love in my life," he said. "What is the secret?" The layman hesitated. "We are just growing," he replied. "We are far from being the beloved fellowship we should be. But if there is a secret I believe it is this: Many people in this service have been helped, either by other people here or by the staff. Of those who have joined this Church during the last ten years, most of them have been brought to us by other members. Many couples here have been helped by other couples to make their marriage sacramental or their parenthood more in harmony with God's will. In the ministry of our Church, alcoholics have found freedom; mentally sick persons have come to know re- lease; the brokenhearted have found the comfort of God; young husbands and wives have found spiritual union in their marriage; parents have seen their children and young people grow under the most helpful spiritual influences. Here religion has become real in everyday terms. The services of this Church touch each person vitally. When we come to worship, it is with love and gratitude and expectation. If there is any secret, that must be it."

Of such is the Kingdom of God. Of such is the fellowship of the True Church. Such is the way to the secret spring.

V

IT CAN BE ACHIEVED

IN THE very hell of war, the True Church was in evidence. No one can read of the resistance of the Dutch church, feel its penitence, its humility, its daring faith, its magnificent loyalty, without a stir of admiration. All through the occupation of Europe in the recent war, there was a remnant that stood fast against tyranny over the souls of men and of nations. The True Church does exist, but its local units are not easy to discover. With our civilization gasping to live, and with our most-prized institutions tottering in the mighty opposing cross-currents of selfish national interests, its influence is not apparent. But let it become suddenly nonexistent and the miracle of its power would be overwhelmingly realized.

Nowhere in any local unit is the True Church given full expression. Most contemporary Churches seek to help their members combine spiritual growth with a devotion to our sensate culture. But in some of these units there is a faithful remnant of those who seek first the Kingdom, who are fully surrendered to the will of God and who spend their lives finding, knowing and revealing Him to others. They may not be the leaders of their group, for they are often the least vocal. They do not parade virtues, nor are they enemies of human impulses. They love the Lord with heart, mind and soul, and their neighbors as themselves. It is these who have a quiet inner core to their living that lights the spark of hope in others, and calls more persons to God than the loquacious efforts of those who talk and do, but who have not sought nor received life eternal.

Similarly, among the clergy in all creeds and faiths, there are those who do not "split" and become both the victim and the carriers of the disease that blights our day: spiritual schizophrenia. They do not try to serve both God and mammon. By the grace of God, they have given all, renouncing the anchors and securities of the material world and surrendering themselves fully to God and His will. They do not exploit their parishioners to please some church dictator in whose beneficent grace their professional future lies. They have gained freedom from all earthly and human dependency by full surrender to God and to the concerns of the spirit. They have risen beyond the need for self-aggrandizement that blurs the sight of men and the vision of God. Through their oneness with God, they are restless and eager to be used to help others come into that saving and life-giving relationship. They have achieved or are, by constant prayer, seeking to achieve the spiritual quality which Aldous Huxley sets forth in these words: "Man's final end, the purpose of his existence, is to love, know and be united with the immanent and transcendent Godhead. And this identification of self with spiritual not-self can be achieved only by 'dying to' selfness and living to spirit."[1]

These are rarely the most widely known members of the clergy, and they usually do not get the large salaries. Since they are removed from the constraint of pleasing large followings, it is therefore easier for them to preach and work for the spiritual growth of the individual. They love their brethren; they pray for them quietly and without fanfare; lives within

[1] *The Perennial Philosophy*, by Aldous Huxley (New York: Harper & Brothers, 1944, 1945), p. 38.

their ministries are changed from earth-centeredness to God; individuals and small groups of persons are growing in the life of spirit. Through their influence, gifted persons are going into Christian service at home and abroad; tithing is abundant; increasing numbers of lay members are brought to share in every phase of the True Church's ministry. While opposition to them grows from the devotees of materialism, their response is one of love and patience.

Unfortunately, many of these true men of God are caught in the system of denominational vested interests. Free within themselves, they are not entirely free to do the will of God because of their denominational allegiance. Many young men who were chaplains, serving without regard to the imprint of any one denomination, upheld the spirit of the ecumenical church in the face of a war against God and its complete denial of love. Now these same young men have returned to face the denominational system of church politics. There are older ministers who bow in shame over the things done in the name of the Lord and within His Church. There are untold numbers within the clergy in whose hearts is the True Church and through whose ministry, if given freedom, it could find full expression.

I

There are some vivid, commanding illustrations of the True Church which encourage us and point the way. Let us observe them.

We find our first illustration in a rural community where, nine years ago, there were five church congregations serving the neighborhood. About one hundred people lived in the village center, but the churches served a rural area covering a township. Today there are two congregations. One has an average attendance of twelve, while the other has nearly four hundred. The latter congregation is composed of four of the former separate denominations.

Before the congregations became federated into one church, each of the five churches was served by a minister who lived outside of the community. Not one of these local congregations had the services of a minister who was present for any purpose other than to preach and to officiate at weddings and funerals. All of the church buildings were inadequate and unattractive. In no one of the churches was there adequate leadership. In this same county there was a consolidated school, staffed by a principal and five teachers, to which all the children came for work in the grades and high school. During the week all of the children shared in the discipline of the mind, but on Sunday morning they were broken up into five little, competing groups and sent to five shabby and unattractive church buildings for spiritual training. Fewer than 30 per cent of the children and 10 per cent of the young people in the school went to any of the churches.

A new minister came to this community to serve one of these churches. According to plan, he was to preach on alternate Sundays both here and in another church in a neighboring community. Seeing the absurdities in the functioning of the divided church, he challenged his people to form one outstanding church to serve the whole area. After six months of conference and discussion, four of the five Protestant churches agreed to federate. Members of the remaining church were also eager to join but, because of strong denominational ties, they were unable to do so.

I asked the minister who was responsible for this vision that led four churches to become one True Church, to make a list of the advantages that have resulted from the action. His list and comments follow:

1. There is enough money to pay, and enough people to challenge full-time seminary-trained ministerial leadership for the community life. Too long, our rural Churches have been stepping stones for the young, the resting place for the unqualified, and the door out for the aged. I believe that the single-churched rural community presents a young minister the greatest opportunity in all Protestantism.

2. The religion of the community hits a higher level of effectiveness in both numbers reached, and quality of work done. Our community has four hundred families. No other church assumes responsibility for three hundred and fifty of these, so our church does. One-fourth of these people are members of the church and Sunday school. Over one-eighth, or about one hundred and sixty people, are at Sunday school and Church on any one Sunday. People of no church and any church come to this community religious institution.

The quality of service rendered is higher because we have enough people to age-group our constituency into departments where we can do specialized work under the supervision of teachers and leaders who are trained for their task. For example, we have agencies such as a daily vacation church school, two young people's organizations, a scout troop, choir, directed church recreation and adult education which is on a par with city church programs.

3. A third advantage is what I have called unified religious personnel; by which I mean that our farm leaders, store operators, public school teachers and other leaders make a tremendous spiritual impact upon the community because they are all working in a single unified community religious program rather than in competition. For example, our Sunday school superintendent is a high school teacher; and about one-half of his Sunday school staff are his public school co-teachers. This panel of community leaders is a

wonderful asset to the rural preacher, for he can relieve himself of much responsibility by passing it on to these co-workers. The faithful service of these loyal leaders makes it possible for their minister to get away from his post many days every month to tell the rural church story. A single church in the place of many does not add leadership; it multiplies leadership.

4. Unified religion makes a maximum use of the community's investment in buildings and equipment. One of our old buildings is now a parish house where comfort and convenience is provided for Sunday school, church, and community organizations. The public school building is used for the vacation church school, ten Sunday school classes, religious drama, and music, and out-of-school athletics. A third building, which is not in use, will probably be moved alongside of the building now used for church, and converted into a religious education plant.

5. The foremost service which the church renders the community is in the area of community public opinion and public behavior. The minister becomes a kind of shepherd of community agencies as well as of the personal life of his flock. You remember that John Frederick Oberlin introduced education, flax, and good roads to the mountaineers of his parish. A full-time resident rural minister must do more than preach; he must take counsel with local business men; teach adult classes in character education, lead the community in wholesome recreation; in short, the rural minister is the spiritual engineer of the community.

Our community has adopted a technique called the community council, through which these various aspects of community life are given spiritual direction. The council is composed of delegates from every community agency. It met last Monday evening. In that circle sat lodge leaders, a businessman, Sunday school superintendent, school superintendent, Farm Bureau head, Parent-Teachers Association head, minister, and two leading laywomen. They arranged a community calendar for six months, then took counsel on a fall community homecoming and festival, and made plans which each leader is taking back to his organization for approval.

This idea of the rural minister being the shepherd of community agencies and the engineer of the community mind is ten-days-by-airplane from the function of the average part-time sectarian preacher. How long will it be before the secretaries of American Protestantism will understand the futility of part-time preachers in competitive churches? A single church in the community increases the influence of the minister and the prestige of Christ.

6. This brings me to the sixth advantage, experimentation or new community approaches. The consolidated rural church has the constituency and the money to apply the most up-to-date methods to the most modern church problems. Under this advantage of experimentation I wish to consider three of our undertakings.

First is recreation. Like most rural communities, no recreation except school athletics, and occasional stale parties, had graced the community. Older young people went to dance halls and to the dogs. Three years ago we began a church program of recreation with the following benefits:

(a) Games of skill replace games of might.

(b) Games of co-operation replace games of competition.

(c) Games of fellowship replace games of hard feeling.

Now our young people play "Weave the Wadmal," "Gustaf's Toast," and games of other lands with the thrill and joy that they play our own American quadrille. The dance hall closed out of business three years ago; and the beer parlor moved out of the township last fall.

Our second experiment is a religious camp project. Our community is not wealthy; but, because we are united, we have been able to get access to a hundred acre woods, erect a lovely cabin with a nice fireplace, and build a large mess hall out of lumber reclaimed from what used to be an eyesore—the old Disciples' Church horse-sheds. We have six five-day camps each summer; for intermediate girls, Boy Scouts, two groups of seniors, older young people, and young mothers. The rural people have been sold on these camps on this theory: a farmer breaks a colt by hitching him to the plow every day for a week, not by hitching him on Sunday forenoons each week. Just so, intensive religious training is most effective. About eighty people attended these local camps last summer. They are our most effective means of building character and creating leadership.

The third experimental project is in the field of adult education. Last month we operated a study group upon the co-operative movement. This was a local advance into the area of community economic redemption. Fourteen post high school young people did twenty hours of class work in addition to home study on this subject.

During the previous winter a co-operative school for young men was held. Nine attended the full five-day session. On the first day they showed the popular attitude of hopelessness about the farm situation in America. As soon as they heard about the Peasant Gospel schools in Japan and the story of Denmark, they became enlivened. A chart of the new producer-consumer society stirred their minds with an endless list of questions. Work committees often slowed up their task because they became so interested in further discussion of some factor regarding co-operation.

The method of learning fluctuated easily between such forms as lecture, debate, panel form, questions, craft and visual education. Songs and jokes were readily used especially at the beginning of meals and lectures. Occasionally the atmosphere became such that prayer was the natural development in the group. The school was said to be the highest form of religious education because the group not only talked co-operation but was, in brief, an actual co-operative community. The ministers deliberately set the stage by practicing sharing and mutual aid throughout the period. Representatives from marketing co-operatives, consumers' co-operatives, credit unions, farm bureaus and county agents, as well as the county FERA rural economics and recreation instructors, gave generously of their time and equipment.

Each person brought produce or money to the extent of $2.25. Some of the boys brought profanity; but they did not use it. Some brought tobacco, but did not smoke. A beer parlor was at hand, but not frequented. Is it possible that undesirable behavior may be corrected by replacing it with creative activity?

I would repeat, these experiments show that there are new approaches to community redemption which come to the rural church when sectarianism is abolished.

One of the former church buildings in this town is now a recreation center. Another is used for children's work. The third has been moved across the road and joined to the fourth building, which together form a sanctuary and a meeting hall for the religious education of young people and adults. There are at present over five hundred members in this federated church. Three hundred and twenty-five of them belong to the federated church itself, while the rest are members of the four units that constitute the federation. It is significant that members give missionary funds not only to the four denominations that make up their federation but also to ecumenical activities locally, in America, and over the world. Their worship sanctuary is within a hundred yards of the consolidated school building. Children and young people go to the same school and share in the same Church. Families who join in various activities of a communal nature share with unity and oneness in worship and in service.

One of the laymen, speaking of the federated church, said:

Before we got together and had one vital church, the churches didn't amount to much in our community. Some of us went out of loyalty and some of us went just because we'd been brought up that way. But whatever our reasons were, church was strictly a Sunday morning proposition. The minister was someone to entertain after church on Sunday and someone we needed in case of funerals and weddings. But now our pastor is part of the way we live. He is not interested in religion that is apart from life. Instead he tries to help us find the meaning of religion in everything we do.

Many of the young people's activities in the community are put on jointly by the Church and the school. Recently, through the vision of the minister and the principal, the young people of high school age were asked to take an area of nontillable land and carry on a program of reforestation. They got the use of a bulldozer and dug out a place for a lake, which they have stocked with fish. They have built lodges where groups can come for picnic suppers. They have built an amphitheatre for public worship. The young people share in service work with various social agencies. While most of them are busy on farms, working in the 4-H Club, they have time to participate in the civic and social activities of their community.

In this community the Church has become a unified True Church. It is a fellowship of the way and it is bringing both families and school into that fellowship.

Here is an answer to the problem of thousands of communities over America that can only afford one church. Rural religion has been pretty largely Protestant. But the Roman Catholic church has observed the failure of Protestants to minister adequately to our great farm areas and men like Bishop Ligutti have recognized that the big reason for the failure of Protestantism is its persistence in maintaining its 252 divisions. In *The Christian Century*, Charles Clayton Morrison said this about Protestantism and its scandalous perpetuation of a divided Church in both small and large communities:

Protestantism, with only twice the Catholic membership, supports 17½ times as many local churches. There would be occasion for satisfaction if there were as many as 230,000 cities, towns, and villages in the length and breadth of this great country, and if these 230,000 Protestant churches were distributed among them all. But this is notoriously not the case. Nearly all these churches exist side by side with other Protestant churches in small and large communities. They are not there because the community needs them, nor because Protestantism needs them, nor because Christianity needs them. They are there because each one of more than 200 denominational "churches" imagines that its peculiar brand of Protestantism ought to be propagated by the organization and maintenance of its own local churches regardless of the effect upon these communities and upon Protestant Christianity as a whole.[2]

Interdenominational competition has become a cancer in the body of the Protestant church. It is indeed fortunate that there are those who recognize the signs of disease. All through New England, and through New York State, Ohio, Indiana, Illinois, Michigan and Wisconsin, there are many federated churches, and the number is growing. While the mere fact that two or more churches get together is no proof that they will be the True Church, it is evidence of growth in love and trust. The federated church is the first step toward a united Church, and is a bulwark to the principle of united nations.

II

Another illustration of the True Church comes from a still smaller rural community in which the only church was a part

[2] Charles Clayton Morrison, *The Christian Century*, June 12, 1946.

of a four-church circuit. To some of the leaders within this church came a vision of a community-centered church with a full-time pastor. For years the services of a minister had been available only every other Sunday and on such special occasions as weddings and funerals. When these laymen approached the denominational representative, he discouraged them. His reason was that they did not have the resources nor the willingness on the part of the people to make possible a church with a full-time minister.

But one layman kept alive his devotion to the idea of one church in a community and kept working at his dream. He was able to enlist the interest of other laymen as well as many of the young people. They wanted their own church; they wanted to fashion it after the apostolic or earlier church. While they wanted it to be a part of the Church Universal, they wanted it to be a church of, by and for the people in their community. While they wanted it to vibrate with the pulse of the whole world, they believed that its program should grow out of the needs of the people and should take its pattern from the community.

Once the decision was reached to have a full-time church with a full-time minister, they faced the problem as to where he would live. No minister had ever resided in that community. Finally, one layman proposed the idea of buying a farm. They presented this idea to the community and within three weeks $7,000 was raised to purchase a farm of ninety acres. The farm house is as good as any in the entire countryside. The plan is for this to be a farm of the church, with the church members cooperating in its maintenance and operation. The minister is not expected to maintain more than his own house and garden, but will work along with members to make the farm a financially sound source of support for the church. It is a venture daring in outline and rich in promise: not to set apart the goals of the spirit from the means of physical livelihood, but to bind them together in theory and practice so that cultivation of the earth and of the life of the spirit becomes a single, all-engrossing project.

These are farm people who expect their minister to guide them not only in building a church that will help them grow spiritually to find a vital and wonderful faith, but also in living that faith in all relations of the business of farming, which is the basis of their lives. They want a church that is centered in worship and one that will fulfill the greatest ministry to their children, young people, and men and women. They want the church building to be a place where boys and girls, young people, and men and women not only grow in the knowledge of God, but build a fellowship in the very light of His love. They want a church that is ready to extend its principles of Christian guidance in such reciprocal ministries as a credit union, a program of health education for boys and girls, and a forum for discussion and solution of farm problems.

Here is a church that will be community-centered in the most fundamental sense. Here is a True Church of the countryside.

III

Let us turn now to a town of twelve hundred for a third illustration of the True Church. Here the Disciples of Christ and Methodist churches had been serving the people of the community, each in its own way, for more than a century. For years they had been competing for allegiance in the village and surrounding territory. The minister of the Methodist congregational has been there seven years, and the young man who ministers to the Disciples of Christ church has been in the community fourteen years.

From the beginning the two ministers had been very friendly, but their churches were competitive. One day when they were playing golf with one of the town's business men, it was suggested that they start a civic club. There was general agreement that a need for such a club existed, but as they talked it over, they became convinced that it should become more than is usually meant by the term, "civic." It should embody, they felt, all community interests—religious, literary, fraternal, educational, patriotic—and should include young people as well as adults in its membership.

As a part of this enterprise, the two clergymen decided that their churches should sponsor some joint activity. Surely, if they could enjoy playing golf together, their congregations could find satisfaction in worshiping together. With this in mind, they began to join in various co-operative projects. Every other Sunday evening a community devotional service of some kind was held. One Sunday evening it was a hymn sing, with a visiting choir or chorus. On another occasion a speaker brought a message, to the combined congregations. Another time there were religious films. Now and then men of the two churches provided the program. Then again, the women, and sometimes the young people.

Community youth meetings were also held every other Sunday evening. The young people assembled at 5:00 P.M., before the general community session. They spent an hour in fellowship, a half hour for refreshments, and closed with an hour of worship and discussion. They met in the two church buildings alternately.

Several years ago the two ministers attended a pastors' conference in the capital city. As they chatted together one night, they wondered if they were going far enough. They asked themselves whether they were not merely touching the edges of co-operative action. They thought and prayed together.

The possibility of having a community church office occurred to them, and with it came the recollection of a vacant second floor room in a building on the main street. The building proved to belong to one of their golf foursome. Following a conference, he agreed to provide the room, rent free, and also to give them light and heat. The post office was located on the first floor of the building, and to have the community church office on the second floor seemed an ideal arrangement.

The project was undertaken. Each church elected two members from its official church board to make up the new community church's board. These four members then elected a fifth, who became the chairman. Laymen contributed three hundred dollars for furnishings. The ministers and their people did the wallpapering and painting of woodwork. They built partitions, bought rugs, tables, desks, chairs and a reading rack. The community church office became a cheerful, attractive headquarters.

Up to this time each minister had had a study in his own home, but neither had an office. Now each had his own office in the community church office. The office was also at disposal for committee and forum meetings. Addressograph and mimeograph equipment and a small printing machine were made available, whereas neither church had even had mimeographing facilities up to that time. For the first time, also, the ministers had a secretary.

The co-operation so hesitantly begun gained momentum. The public school building has now been brought into use for a daily vacation Bible school in which both churches join. The pastors drive school buses and transport children from outlying sections of the community. In 1946, over two hundred and fifty children were enrolled, with twenty-five adult members on the staff—an unusually large vacation school for a town of twelve hundred. At this writing, both pastors are teaching religion in the public schools of the town, with classes on a voluntary basis.

During the vacation period, the two ministers agreed that one or the other would be in town all of the time. One was on vacation in July, the other in August. With the two congregations meeting together in the summer, the problem of supply preachers has been solved.

In a recent conversation with these two ministers, I was encouraged to learn that they are now carrying on one program for children in the community church. All children up through the sixth grade meet in one church building for church school, while the junior and senior high groups, the young people, and adults meet for their church school in the building of the other church.

There is now a united men's brotherhood, to which men of both churches belong. There is one women's guild. They are working toward one outstanding junior high school program for Sunday night; one for senior high school; one for those out of high school, and one for young adults. Basically, the only thing that still remains separate is the morning worship service.

At the end of the first year of the plan's operation, attendance at the morning church service increased fourfold. Their budgets increased three times; and their missionary giving to their own denominations and to interdenominational activities was quadrupled.

When I asked the two ministers how the plan is working out,

one of them said, "Too well. I never seem to get my own work done anymore." Further conversation with both men indicated that perhaps that is just what the situation needed. The new community works so well that the institution becomes secondary. Union and fellowship, oneness in God, a common aspiration to His Kingdom—these are the things that are most required. Here in this town, two churches of different denomination have found Christian oneness with diversity of expression. In their fellowship the concept of a world community gains meaning.

In speaking to one of the laymen in the community, I received this comment: "Until our two churches became one in spirit, and until they got away from fighting each other, the Church was only on the edge of things. Now it is becoming the inspiration of all community life."

As I talked with other individuals in the town, I was inspired by reactions such as these: "Once we fought to get a new family into our church; now we are interested in getting all families into *the* Church. We are all a part of the Church. Some of us meet one place for worship and some at the other, but in all of our activities we are one fellowship." And again, "Before we got together, our ministers had to take care of a great many details that a secretary could easily have handled, but we felt that we did not have the money. Now, since we have gone together in one office, we not only have enough money to pay our ministers and increase our missionary giving and improve our equipment, but we have enough more to provide the ministers with an efficient secretary." Further, "Our ministers are looking forward to having, in the near future, a full-time woman to work with our children. And later on, a full-time leader for our young people." The ministers themselves reported that within the near future they are going to employ a full-time minister of music to train choirs for both church services and for their united meetings, and to teach the value of religious music in all of their work.

The superintendent of schools said of this effort: "It has been encouraging to me to see that people who unquestioningly share in and believe in the public school are able also to federate and unite their efforts in worship and religion."

Here, in this small town, a new unit of the True Church is born, a new fellowship of the way. Here again is a fulfillment of the dream of unity in God.

From all sides we hear the plea for religious unity, for the removal from the Church of those divisive, competitive barriers that result in its ineffectiveness and impotence. For many years there has been in the National Cathedral in Washington, D.C. an annual conference of Christian unity, but it has never yet got beyond the stage of talk and into the sphere of action. It is true that here and there two denominations may get together, but is this the answer? There are now more people in the Methodist and Baptist denominations than in the Roman Catholic church in America. Does the answer to the divided Church in the local community lie in the strengthening of denominations? Is there any real solution to the problem of the divided Church except unification?

Here are verdicts from a number of people with regard to the need for union:

As soon as every person in every nation begins to understand that it is possible that he can be bombed out of existence from any other point on this planet, then people might decide to act as if all men were brothers. It is not a wholly pleasant thought that the pilot, the bombardier, and the airplane designer may be more potent factors than the somewhat divided doctrines of religious teachers in producing a sense of unity among mankind. But the ways of the Lord and the devil never have been easy to divine.[3]

It will require a united fellowship of Christians to combat the hostile ideologies which degrade men and turn earth in shambles, and ideologies which ignore God and leave man orphaned and helpless. . . . Only by a united witness of what God has convinced us in His saving truth, will it be possible to save the world. . . . Nor can our present divided Church supply the fellowship necessary to build a brotherhood of nations. We rejoice in the happy phrase "The United Nations"; it presages intelligently conceived common action against a more menacing foe. Why not "The United Church," conserving the tradition and types of witness and worship which have grown up through our separated histories, but conserving them in a reunited church.[4]

Now, when nations are threatened with disunity, is the time for "the followers of Christ" to rise above their sectarian divisions and show a united front. The issues which divide the Christian Church are, after all, only family differences, and the family of God must set an example for the family of nations. If we who call God Father cannot sit down in common council to plan cooperative action, is it surprising that governments which deny God hold aloof from the United Nations? A united Church, praying and pleading for the United Nations, would release the power of Him who is able to do exceeding abundantly above all that we ask or think. Vague talks about human brotherhood and reverence for personality are not enough in the present hour.[5]

Certainly our divided Churches cannot deal with the kind of a world we have on our hands today. We see that world tortured and afflicted by divisions; the divisions that arise out of conflicting

[3] James P. Gifford, "Groups and Economic Advantages" in *Civilization and Group Relationships* (New York: Harper & Brothers, 1945), p. 106.

[4] Henry Sloan Coffin in a statement at a meeting of the New York Presbytery, Spring, 1946.

[5] Dr. Ralph W. Sockman, in a statement at Christ Church, Methodist, New York City. Quoted from *The New York Times*, April 1, 1946.

political and economic philosophies; divisions between nations; divisions between racial groups. . . . Here, as I see it, is the challenge that God today is laying upon all our Churches. If we are to meet this challenge we need one another today as never before and we shall need to learn to do things together. For brave and adventurous souls this may be an exciting and thrilling time in which to live but I do not see how any thoughtful Christian can look out upon the world, as we know it today, without being afraid; afraid for ourselves, and afraid for our Churches as the medium through which God must work. If those Churches, or if we, as members of those Churches fail God today we are going to have something for which to answer.[6]

IV[7]

We have seen illustrations of the growth of the True Church in two farming areas and in a rural town. We come now to a picture of the True Church as it has developed in an urban area.

In 1909, in a suburb of a city, a Sunday school was formed in a school building. In 1910 a community census was taken in this suburb, with a majority of the people registering their interest in the Congregational church. The church that was subsequently formed in the community became a unit in the Congregational denomination. In 1911 the cornerstone was laid for a building in which this church was to meet. Through the influence of one of the great Congregational leaders, the church became a community church in 1915. This leader, as well as many of the church members, was able to foresee that if they

---

[6] Rt. Rev. Charles K. Gilbert, in a speech delivered before the St. George Association of New York on Sunday, March 24, 1946. Quoted from *The New York Times*, March 25, 1946.

[7] Quoted material in this section is from a pamphlet published by this church and is used by permission of the board of trustees.

remained a denominational unit, other denominations would soon invade the community with the inevitable result of division and competition between them.

A community-centered church is a church made up on a multi-denominational or interdenominational pattern, being constituted of people of all faiths. It is an entity in itself and bears only a relationship of love to other church units in the body of Christ. Community-centered churches may be federated, they may be union churches, or they may be identified with one denomination.

The community church described here now has a membership of 3,475 people representing thirty-two different denominations. It is affiliated with no denomination. It was formed with this creed:

I believe in the Living God, the Father of all mankind.

I believe in Jesus Christ, as He is revealed to me as the Lord and Saviour of my life and of the world.

I accept as the guiding principles of my life and conduct the teachings of Jesus, who when asked, "What is the great commandment?" said, "Thou shalt love the Lord thy God with all thy heart, and with all thy soul and with all thy mind. And the second is like unto this: Thou shalt love thy neighbor as thyself."

Into its thirty-year history as a community church has gone the concerted effort of staff and membership toward the development of a religious institution truly community-wide in scope. Its activities stem from community needs and follow the community pattern. Its success in achieving its aims can be measured in such definite terms as a decreased rate of juvenile delinquency. Its influence is not only felt within the bounds of its own suburban area, but also extends into the adjacent city.

In this church, the Sunday services of worship are the spiritual hub of widespread activities. Worship is central to every aspect of the church program. The regular Sunday services of the church include an early service of communion, two morning worship services, and an afternoon vesper service. These it seeks to make so vital that the power of worship will be carried over into the everyday life of each family and individual that shares in its fellowship. Through prayer circles and devotional meetings during the week, it refreshes and renews its inspiration.

One of the distinctive factors of its fellowship is that it does not specialize in any age. It is as interested in children as it is in adults, and its program provides resources for the spiritual enrichment and growth of members of all ages.

The church employs a director of Christian Education whose responsibility is both to child and parent. It conducts a day nursery and a day kindergarten five mornings a week, both with full-time trained leaders who are equipped to counsel mothers on problems of child rearing. In the summer there are day camps for the smaller children, and a week's camp for the older children. There are special Sunday services for all children, including a junior church, and a children's choir.

With a membership of eight hundred young people, its youth activities are diverse and varied. This church says of its interest in young people:

We conceive of no higher imperative than that of faithfully bestowing upon each one all of the richness and meaning of the spiritual birthright that should be theirs. We offer each young person a faith, and reasons for that faith. We show him that the universe is dependable and reveals the workings of a Planner; we teach him that his body is the temple of the Holy Spirit; that personality is sacred; that all men are worthy of his love because of their creation.

For its high school and college groups, the church provides worship services which the young people themselves plan and in which they participate. Its young people's choir takes part in regular worship services. It has Sunday evening discussion groups that follow a stimulating, carefully planned year's curriculum. On Saturday nights, the church house is open to its young people for a social evening of games, dancing and crafts, and holiday parties are annual affairs. The church has special training classes in which it prepares its youth for church membership. It has a summer camp program for young people. It organizes groups of young men and women to share in the work of settlement houses and other social agencies. It has recently begun a series of dramatic radio broadcasts for youth.

For young adults there are both separate and joint meetings for men and women. There are circles of young couples who meet in one another's homes for fellowship and group study. For the young unmarried adults, the church gives instruction in preparation for marriage. For those who are parents, it offers counseling on child problems.

The men and women of the church are asked to take an active part in planning its work and to serve actively on its committees and boards. There are women's guilds, a men's brotherhood, and Bible study classes for both. There is a world fellowship group and a social action group. An important aspect of the church's adult program is its use of lay members to visit prospective church members, to conduct training programs for new members, and to make sure that new members are welcomed and assisted in finding their place in the whole church program.

The church looks upon itself not as an institution set apart from other community institutions, but as an integral part of the neighborhood. There are two different school systems in the community, and the church and schools work as a team. The two school superintendents are on the Program and Policy Committee of the church. Ninety-two per cent of the children and young people that go to one school share in the fellowship of this church, and of the other school, 40 per cent of the children and 80 per cent of the high school students. Within the area of the latter school there are two other Protestant churches. It is the policy of the community church to encourage people living near those two churches to go there. The three church units work in co-operation and in love.

In case a child or youth needs special help, the leadership of the school and church together pool their resources with those of the parents to solve the problem. The various character-building agencies, such as scouts and camp fire groups, center their activities within the community church building. The church building is the center where many other interests that are devoted to the guidance of life and its enrichment are hallowed and given spiritual purpose. The baccalaureate services of the two schools are held in its sanctuary. Outstanding student leaders in the schools are trained in its camps, and within the church program. Most of the teachers of the schools share their religious life together in the church. The two schools, once competitive, have grown together because their young people go to one church and share in its spiritual purpose. Through the initiative and financial support of the church, weekday schools of religion that reach 99 per cent of the children through the first six grades have been made possible in both schools.

Off to the side of this community there is a negro settlement of about three hundred people. When the denomination of which they are a part sold their church building, they came for their worship and activities to the community church building.

When distance made the plan impractical for permanent use, both white and negro congregations joined together to build a church for the negro settlement. Young people of both groups worked in digging the basement. Deacons of both churches worked at the actual building. The negro church is now complete, and the two churches are linked together in a spirit of brotherhood and co-operation.

The community church has sought to minister also to the larger neighborhood that is the city. Eleven years ago, the church was challenged by the judge of the juvenile court to do something about a district from which 90 per cent of the city's delinquents came. The young people of the church and their minister spent many Sunday afternoons visiting homes in the area, finally sponsoring a party for boys and girls of the district. More than two hundred came. Their response and their interest were so enthusiastic that it was decided to launch a settlement house to minister to the district. Through the co-operation of a minister and his congregation, a house was made available in the midst of the needy area. A woman from the community church became the settlement's first staff member. The program is growing rapidly and the settlement house is now included in the regular community fund. Last year, instead of 90 per cent of the delinquents coming from that area, fewer than 18 per cent of them came from within the parish of the settlement house. Much of the volunteer leadership in the settlement house comes from people of the community church. There is an interchange of real fellowship between the two.

The counseling ministry of the church is made use of by people from all over the city. Counsel is given on personal problems, parent-child difficulties, marital bafflements, vocational guidance and job problems. There is a ministry to returned veterans. The offices of the church are available at all times in case of death or other crises.

When a movement was begun for the establishment of a council of churches in the city, the community church entertained the first group of representatives to consider the council. It provided office facilities and postage for the first year, while the groundwork for the council was being laid. With the council now in its second year, the community church is not only the largest financial contributor to its maintenance, but is ready to participate in further efforts to make a united church possible within the larger neighborhood that is the city.

Five mornings a week there is a devotional radio program broadcast from the sanctuary of the community church. In it no mention is made of the church. It reaches children in public school and high school, people in institutions, people in all walks of life and of all ages. It is a definite daily ministry to the spiritual life not only of the city but of a large part of the state as well.

The board of women in the community church has set up a visitation committee to minister to older women in all parts of the city who are neglected. There is a group of men who have dedicated themselves to a similar service for men.

The church works with the various social agencies. When boys or girls from the neighborhood get into difficulty in court, they are assigned to the church. The church works with the family and children's bureau in ministering to families all over the city; in giving guidance to unwed mothers; in the important matter of adoption and in special charity work. It works closely with the probate court in cases of mental breakdown and with the court of domestic relations in assisting families threatened with a break. Its young people take part in the corrective program of the bureau of juvenile delinquency.

Here is no mere Christian Church, but a church of practicing Christianity. Here is not only a house of God, but a home of God and of man. Long past the experimental stage, it has been for many years a symbol of true fellowship. It has weathered the most stringent test of its efficacy; it has continued to grow.

There is a growing number of community churches in suburbs and neighborhoods of cities all over the country. They are of the three kinds previously mentioned: interdenominational, bearing no relationship to any one particular denomination; multi-denominational, of which there are only a few examples, in which all of the denominations represented in the membership are recognized; or of a third type in which the church belongs to one denomination but provides freedom for all forms of religious expression. There are many of this type. Unfortunately, there are too few denominations whose doctrinal structure will allow freedom for forms of religious expression other than their own. Therefore, this type of church is not possible in all places.

In some places the community church is known as a union church. There are many such union churches in New England. The number of community churches is also growing in the South, in the Middle West and throughout the West. There are arguments against the community church, some of which are well taken. We shall look at some of these objections and evaluate them.[8]

One of the criticisms made of the pure community church and of community-centered churches is that they are not spiritually centered. This point may be justified in some instances, but cannot the same criticism be made of hundreds of denominational churches which are the victims of a bondage to a building and to an hour

---

[8] Quotation that follows is from an article entitled "The Community Church" written by the author for the Spring, 1946, issue of *Christendom*, vol. XI, no. 2, pp. 188-198.

a week? If a community church achieves the real functions of the Church of Christ, its opportunity to become spiritually centered is greater than if people come together for an hour a week which is their only basic common experience. What do we call "spiritually-centered?" In the parable of the Good Samaritan, religion is found to be an answer to human needs; in the story of the Last Judgment, it was those individuals who answered the cry of the imprisoned, the hungry and the lonely who were actually responding to the call of God. The church answering such needs in community life is vitally alive and spiritually-centered. . . .

Whether a community church is spiritual is dependent upon the vision of the leadership and the long-range guidance and planning. The possibilities of living out the all-inclusive love of God are infinitely greater in a community church than in a denominational church that includes only a small percentage of the people and that inevitably finds itself competing and that gets its program directives imposed upon it from an overhead organization.

Another charge levied against the pure community church is that it is apt to be provincial in its point of view. This is a definite danger; but it is paralleled by the danger on the part of the denominational church that it fails to see the total community and its problems. The denominational church in the local community is in danger of thinking of segments of that community. Because of this, the whole matter of group tensions, of relations of capital and labor, of race tensions is usually outside the church's consciousness. If the community church maintains a relationship with the great interdenominational agencies and if its leadership is sensitive to the challenge of the world church and of world needs, then it can easily be saved from the danger of the provincial point of view.

To overcome the danger of provincialism, since the community churches have found it difficult to win a place in the present organization of interdenominational agencies, there has been formed a very informal Association for Community-Centered Churches on a national basis. The leaders are determined not to become a denomination. The Association will not ordain ministers, but expects to secure the ordination of suitable candidates through existing units of well-recognized denominations. It will never have its own missionary program, since the World Council of Churches, the International Missionary Council, the Federal Council of Churches, and other interdenominational agencies can serve as its channels, and since many outstanding missionary efforts are now interdenominational.

In Ohio there is an Ohio Association for Community-Centered Churches; there is one in Western New York, one in New England, and one around Chicago. It is the intention to keep this fellowship very informal and to get local leaders to pool their experiences rather than to have a large paid staff. This new movement of community-centered churches is unique in its approach to church union. It seeks to go into local communities and guide groups of community-minded lay people, both from the churches and from the un-churched, who will study the community and its significance and discover the procedures and next steps in a program and ministry seeking to meet those needs. If no church is there, a church may come into being but only when the people themselves want it and will help shape it and determine it. If there are now competing churches there and the people decide to unite them into a federated or union church, they will be guided in so doing; and it is hoped that the denominations will be so interested in achieving the most successful ministry of Christ to persons that they will be saved from trying merely to protect the units of their institution which may be involved.

This informal association will be a way by which the orphaned churches, the pure community churches and the federated churches, can have a sense of fellowship together until such time when the denominations discover a way to give them leadership without absorbing them or destroying their community-centered quality.

Another criticism directed at the community church is that its leadership has no standards; that the pure community church is often a place for the untutored and the reactionary religionist to hold forth. One answer to this criticism might be that most of the weird types of religion are denominationally organized, and that many other irregular congregations not at present related to any larger fellowship aspire to become denominations. Most of the irregularity occurs within the denominational pattern. However, the community churches do need assistance. One of the motivating purposes of the organization of the Association for Community-Centered Churches was to help pure community churches or federated churches to find suitable ministers. Others are: to guide those churches in finding materials and resources, to help their ministers grow in the steps of building the beloved community—an emphasis, incidentally, almost entirely overlooked in the theological seminaries—and to provide other necessary resources to the local church. The time is here to enlist strong young men for these pure community churches. Up to this time no one has done it. For this reason the Association has come into being. Any time another agency created by the denominations will do it, in harmony with the fullest ecumenical idea and with the fullest loyalty to the community, the Association is ready to go out of existence.

Another objection to the community church often made is that no single local church can provide for the variety of religious experiences of different people. The writer questions the truth of this. In any city one can find Methodists who refuse to go to one particular Methodist Church but are perfectly happy to go to another. The same is true of Episcopalians, Lutherans, and the other denominations. . . .

When Protestants come to the place where they have a church for each neighborhood, those who do not like the particular program that grows out of the needs and interests of the people and the nature of the leadership of the staff will then have to go to some unit of the church in a nearby neighborhood. This necessity, however, will be reduced to a minimum if it is a church of, by, and for the people rather than the church of a minister and for a few members whose program is handed down from the top.

V

There are a few widely known examples of denominational churches, serving a whole city and at the same time ministering to their immediate neighborhood, which have real elements of the True Church within them. One of these has a Baptist heritage, yet it is ecumenical in almost every sense. Its main weakness is that most of its ministry is carried out by a paid staff so that there is limited participation in service by its members. Still this church is a bright light that illumines a great city, and persons go there to worship from all over the nation and the world. Its influence is as broad as the world and it is of equal inspiration to the clergy and to laymen.

In this same great city there is another church carrying the name of its denomination which ministers to the whole city in a similar manner. But it makes a unique, full-time contribution to children and youth from the slums. It has the rarest combination of wealth and poverty of any church, perhaps, in America. It is great with the commandment, "Inasmuch as ye have done it unto the least of these, ye have done it unto Me," and it measures up as few do to the admonition, "Love the Lord thy God with all thy mind, heart and soul."

In another city there is a denominational church that also has the guiding spirit of the True Church. It is a seven-day church, serving a large city and its suburbs and ministering with eagerness to the neighborhood where it is located. It has three services Sunday morning: an early worship service for leaders in the church school and for the public, a two-hour church school, and a second preaching service. Sunday evening there is a vital program for youth and young adults, followed by another church service.

On the staff of the church is a social worker who guides the members in an intensive ministry of service. There is a full-time director of a theater where young adults can grow in the dramatic arts. There is a day nursery with a regular program for children after school and on Saturday. It is a large church but has a small staff because the members carry a large part of the ministry. This church has one of the most effective church schools in the country, with all of the leadership voluntary except for the associate pastor. Though a part of one of the largest denominations, it is ecumenical to its very heart.

We write of one other denominational church, which carries the name of the avenue on which it is located in a large city. In all references I have heard made to this church, I have never heard its denomination mentioned. Its Sunday program is one of the most spiritual and life-changing of any church in the nation. It has two consecutive church services each Sunday morning, with a two-and-a-half hour church school for children, and an hour-and-a-half church school for youth and adults. Sunday evening it has one of the most far-reaching youth programs in America. The program includes students of junior and senior high age, college people, and young adults. The average attendance is over five hundred. They have a two-and-a-half hour program, including supper, social fellowship, class discussion and a service in the sanctuary. It is in this church that the University of Life was conceived and found to be so successful.

With one exception, the members of these churches are very active in all aspects of the church's life. In all there is a deep spiritual tone. In all there are many small groups or units that meet to sustain the spiritual growth of individual members. In all, the world mission of the Church is vivid. Such churches that serve a whole city obviously cannot have the same meaning for the individual as a community church that is made up of persons from a given neighborhood. At best their congregations are together only once a week. The True Church is always located as close as possible to the place where its people live. If and when there is a single Protestant church for each public school district, then will the Protestants have their great opportunity to become leaders of the True Church.

It is not possible to find adequate illustrations of the True Church for nowhere is it fully realized. But we have seen many local churches that are becoming the True Church as we have attempted to define it. While only a few such illustrations are described here, there are many more scattered over the nation. As we look at these, which we have described, we find some conclusions worthy of note.

1. In all of the illustrations the program of the Church rests on the conviction that the ministry of the True Church must extend into all the relations of life. The True Church does not cease to exist with the close of the morning service, nor is it circumscribed by the limits of its building. The True Church is in the home with the housewife, in the factory with the wage earner, in the schoolroom with the child. Wherever people are, there is the True Church.

2. The church programs, moreover, have been broad in concept, covering a wide range of activities. The True Church seeks to help individuals find the will of God and live by it, believing that emotion and conduct cannot be separated. If worship can have meaning only when it is a part of everyday living, then the program of the True Church has real significance only when it includes all the experiences of everyday life.

3. It is evident, further, that there is a growing need to make the church fellowship identical with the neighborhood fellowship. Those can best worship together who work and play together.

4. Another factor in evidence is that the True Church is devoted to all ages. It ministers to the individual from birth until death, and to groups of all ages and at all levels of maturity. Its ministry is not the victim of a schedule or a building, but covers the whole week.

5. Another tendency in evidence is a growth away from the denominational label, and toward the Church of the Living God. Within the True Church is the answer to the prayer of our Lord "that they all may be one."

In the preceding chapter I described what was called a visit to the secret spring. This chapter but sketches the behavior of those who have visited the spring, and departed refreshed. For such the Church is inseparable from community living; the Church is identical with God's will made manifest.

IT CALLS FOR NEW PREACHING

A FOREMOST medical missionary of the world, Sir Wilfred Grenfell of Labrador, was launched in his dramatic career by a sermon delivered by Dwight L. Moody. John Wesley, founder of Methodism, heard a sermon in a London meetinghouse and "felt his heart strangely warm within him." He subsequently fostered a fellowship that has resulted in one of the largest denominations in the world. William Booth listened to a sermon in a Methodist chapel and started the Salvation Army, which is active today in more than ninety countries. Those who preach the ineffectiveness of preaching controvert the facts of religious experience.

Two of Chicago's leading educational institutions resulted from the stimulus growing out of sermons. Northwestern University came into being as a struggling school on the frontier back in 1851, after Orington Hunt, a layman, heard a fiery sermon on the need for Christian education among pioneers. The Illinois Institute of Technology, one of the three greatest in America, was the product of a million dollar sermon by Dr. Frank W. Gunsaulus, pastor of Central Church, who said that he could launch a much-needed technical school for that amount. Philip D. Armour, the packer, writing out his check for one million dollars, gave it to the minister and told him to go ahead. Gunsaulus started the Armour Institute of Technology.

In the summer of 1946, ten thousand people assembled in Adrian, Michigan, to give away one hundred thousand dollars.

All of this resulted from a stirring sermon preached by a young student minister in the Friends Meeting House at Tecumseh, Michigan, on September 22, 1940. He had exhorted the congregation to bear much fruit as Christians—"That means not only helping people into heaven," he said, "but also helping them here on earth. We must preach the word of God and serve Christ by caring for the hungry, the needy, and the despairing. Why shouldn't we do it now?"

One of his hearers, Perry Haden, a miller, planted a cubic inch of wheat—350 grains—on a plot of ground four by eight feet. When he harvested it the next season, he sold one-tenth, gave the proceeds to the church, and planted nine-tenths. This he repeated each year with astounding results. Other farmers joined in the project, and Henry Ford donated the use of some land. The next year five hundred bushels were sold and the money given to the church, and five thousand bushels were distributed among farmers for planting. This year, the crop was expected to yield $100,000 for Christian service, and great throngs gathered at Adrian to celebrate the amazing "Lord's Acre" movement that originated from the planting of a cubic inch of grain.

The most influential piece of literature in history is the Sermon on the Mount. It is the eternal gospel. Within it is formulated the wisdom of the ages regarding the life of the spirit. It holds the secret of the soul's growth in individual and in collective living. It is the description of the way, the illumination of the truth, the explanation of life.

These are graphic illustrations, indicating something of the potentialities of the sermon and of preaching. However, as is clearly implied throughout the pages of this book, preaching is by no means the minister's whole task. His responsibility is to direct all the aspects of the Church's ministry, and his opportunity is to guide the growth of the beloved community so that increasing numbers of individuals will give witness, share, and lead others to God and into His way of life. But once or twice a week, as the members of the fellowship come together to worship, to review progress, to set themselves new tasks, to make new dedications, to envision new frontiers of action, the sermon has a vital part to fulfill in the life of the Church.

It is important that laymen as well as preachers study the preaching ministry of the Church. The True Church calls for a new type of preaching that will only come as laymen sense its need and insist on its realization. This new preaching will take place mainly in the pulpit and in the regular service of worship of the Church. But the minister may also preach over the radio; he will guide services of memory, and conduct wedding ceremonies. While in this chapter we are concerned mainly with his preaching in the pulpit, we will seek specific principles to guide the minister in other areas where preaching has a special function.

I

What is the nature of preaching in the contemporary Church? How effective is it? Let us first look into the message of present-day preaching.

The message of the pulpit varies in content and in emphasis. Some sermons center in the scriptures; others are experience-centered, in the sense that they deal with life. Some are doctrinal, others are ethical. Some are theological, and an increasing number are psychological. Some sermons center in faith; few put the emphasis upon works. In the words of Dr. Paul Ramsey, some are vertical, pointing God-ward. Others are horizontal, reaching out to the concerns and needs of men.[1]

Some of the messages are personal and some are social. Some center in the individual and his concerns; others center in the community and its needs, in the world and its problems. There are sermons which promote and foster the Church or Synagogue as an institution, publicizing its interests and advocating its enterprises; other sermons are concerned with the spiritual invisible Church and its ministry to the needs of people. The implication of some sermons is that the Church as an institution is the most important thing, and under this guise the Church often exploits for its own sake. Other sermons echo the deep agonizing cry of humanity's needs, and are rich with passion in the constant search for the gift of God's grace.

Some sermons are timely; others are timeless. Some center in the present; in others throbs the pulse of eternity. Some deal with life on this earth; others give major attention to life after death. Some sermons are positive, built on the assurance of God's love; others are negative, motivated by the fear of His retribution.

In the Protestant church there are all these types of sermons represented. In the more conservative denominations, the second coming of Christ is preached and the emphasis is chiefly on hell as a punishment for wrongdoing and on heaven as a reward for the good life. Sermons in these groups are centered more in doctrine, they are more theological, they deal with atonement. They stress other-worldly goals rather than living here and now. In the more liberal churches, sermons are more psychological —there is less emphasis upon the doctrines of the cross, of immortality, and of the sacraments of the Church. Emphasis is

[1] Dr. Paul Ramsey, *Social Action*, October 15, 1946.

rather on how to live by the criterion Jesus gives in the 25th Chapter of Matthew, "Inasmuch as ye have done it unto one of the least of these. . . ." Many liberal ministers feel that the Sermon on the Mount itself is psychological rather than theological, dealing with the theory that if men are right in their relationships with one another, they will inevitably grow in right relationship with God.

In between the ultraconservative and the extreme liberal there is a wide range of emphasis. What might be termed the "average minister"—the one who is fundamentally evangelical and yet has a liberal tendency—preaches a sermon in which he attempts to dress up theological doctrine with a modicum of psychological appeal, and to interpret ethical precept in somewhat hazy terms of social service. In the sermons of both the average and extremely liberal minister there is a tendency toward seeking the solution of personal problems and toward meeting great social needs.

The Pulpit, and *The Pulpit Digest*, periodicals of contemporary preaching, invite ministers of all the Protestant faiths— the most conservative and the most liberal—to submit their sermons. The September, 1946, issue of *The Pulpit* shows an interesting variety of sermon topics: "Is It God's Will?"—"My Father Is a Worker"—"When Faith Becomes a Way"—"Putting Reality into Religion"—"Some Unfinished Business"—"The Church and the City"—"Jesus and Labor." Judging from these titles, some of them are theological, some psychological. One is sociological—"The Church and the City"; one deals with an economic issue—the relationship of labor with the Church.

I recently consulted three ministers who are in touch with preaching throughout the nation. When asked this question, "What are the trends in preaching?" one of these nationally known men answered: "There is a definite trend toward the theological, away from the psychological." The second felt that there is a trend toward more doctrine, on the one hand, and, on the other hand, an effort to promote a more vital Christian relationship in all areas of living. The third minister made this reply: "Ministers are increasingly shying away from the controversial issues—more and more preaching inoffensive sermons dealing with questions of faith, theology and personal living, showing little tendency toward facing such mighty social conflicts as the clash between capital and labor, the breach between the minority groups, the breakdown of the family, the emasculation of our democratic form of government. They tend to make the Church a dangerous defender of the evils in our present way of life."

A survey of a recent volume compiled from sermons of a representative group of Protestant, Catholic and Jewish leaders leads the writer to the conclusion that the judgment of the third minister is true, although there are evidences of truth in the other two conclusions as well. On examining the preaching of the Roman Catholic church, I conclude that its emphasis is largely doctrinal—interpreting the Church, its function, its teachings, its sacraments, its beliefs, and its basic assumption that it is the only divine Church. Its position is definite, however, in denunciation of contemporary secularisms as they are conceived by the Catholic church—the evil of birth control, the evils of the modern motion picture, the sins of marrying outside of the Church and of failing to attend the church services. The Roman Catholic church seems to be much more outspoken about the conflict between capital and labor than is the Protestant church. It is making much greater progress in the area of racial conflict, for in many instances there are both colored and white people belonging to the same church. Due to its administrative structure, it is much more aggressive in political action and much more persistent in such forms of social service as hospitals, settlement houses, social work and relief activities.

Without question, the worshiper in the Catholic church accepts more seriously the dictum of his priest than does the Protestant receive his minister's guidance. The Catholic church is built on the authoritarian principle, while the theory of the Protestant church is that the individual is his own priest before God. The Protestant acts on the principle that he is free to seek the truth. The natural result is that the pulpit of the Protestant church will be less effective in influencing the behavior of its people than is that of the Catholic church, unless its preaching can reach a high permanent level of inspirational appeal. It should be noted here that in all the leading democratic nations, there are more Protestants than Catholics.

The type and influence of preaching in the Jewish Synagogue is perhaps somewhere between these two. In the orthodox Synagogue, preaching is more doctrinal; in the liberal Synagogue, it is more psychological and sociological.

In the radio pulpit of all faiths the emphasis is pretty evenly divided among the doctrinal, theological and personal. Very few sermons deal with controversial issues. In a study of a volume of radio sermons given in Wichita, Kansas, in 1944, it was interesting to see that not one of the sermons dealt with major social issues such as world peace, the racial question and economic problems, nor even with such a vital concern as adequate housing.

What can be said of the effectiveness of contemporary sermons? Do they justify the importance of their position in the work of the Church? This is an interesting question.

I have consulted five hundred ministers of all faiths on their allocation of time to planning the church service and to preparing the sermon. Some of them report that they plan to spend one hour of preparation for each minute they preach. Reports from all five hundred preachers indicate a wide range—from 10 to 90 per cent—in the amount of time devoted to the sermon, the pastoral prayer, and the planning of the worship service. The average is 35 per cent, approximately one-third of the minister's total hours of work.

The average theological seminary majors in training men to preach, conceiving of the Church as centered in the pulpit. These five hundred preachers reported that less than 10 per cent of the curriculum emphasis in seminary training was given to ways of organizing a vital parish ministry such as that outlined in Chapter II. All of them agreed that they were taught a theology, but stated that they received little or no preparation for leading people to a vital faith and giving them the passion to live by it. Similarly, most local church budgets are spent on the hour of worship. Compare what the average church spends on its ministry to children and on its ministry to adults.

With all of this emphasis on preaching, does it command an audience? Does it appeal? Does it change lives and foster growth? The five hundred ministers reported that the average regular attendance in their churches is 30 per cent of the membership; that out of each hundred members, they can expect only thirty to be present on a given Sunday. Three of the leading preachers in America, in conversation with the author, once agreed that approximately 5 per cent of the membership of contemporary Protestant churches is truly sincere, and that an additional 5 per cent participates regularly in the life of the church. A group of representative chaplains reported that only 15 per cent of Protestant and Jewish servicemen attend chapel regularly, compared with 85 per cent regular attendance on the part of Roman Catholics.

It is not easy to preach today. People have grown accustomed to more graphic means of portraying experience and idea. They go to movies, where there is action and emotional appeal. They read the headlines and the funnies in the newspapers. They listen to dramatic radio programs where the skill of producer and performer presents and interprets ideas without demanding much thought on the part of the listener.

When the minister stands before his congregation, he faces persons of all ages from adolescence upward. If his church is located in a city or a town, he faces persons from all walks of life and from all economic levels. He faces some few intellectuals who prefer to think for themselves, and many who do comparatively little thinking and who live mainly by their emotions. He faces persons who work with ideas and others who work with their hands. He faces Republicans and Democrats and free political thinkers. The majority of his congregation is made up of people who are against change, who think longingly of the good old days, whose vision is pretty much limited to the immediate community where they live.

The most common lay criticisms of contemporary preaching— and these have been leveled at the preaching of the writer as well—have been along the following lines:

1. It is the feeling of many laymen that sermons are not interesting. They do not strike at the heart of life. Sermons either touch the sphere of everyday living only tangentially, or devote themselves entirely to the intangible and the abstract. They do not speak to the individual. They fail to hold his interest and to quicken his thought. They are too dry or too sentimental. They

either assume that the listener lives only by his intellect or solely by his emotion. They lack warmth; they are inhuman. They are too often not words of life or, as Job said, not "words that keep men on their feet."

2. Laymen express the feeling that most sermons do not start where the laymen are. They are more likely to start where the minister is in his own thinking or in the borrowed thinking of a recently-read book.

3. They feel that the language of most sermons is stilted and that ideas are clothed in obscure phrases.

4. Many laymen consider that most sermons are a rehashing of old topics and that the listener knows what the conclusion will be when he hears the sermon's title.

5. Some laymen feel that too often the preacher is not a good speaker. Unnatural voices are common. Pious speech abounds. They feel that the preacher lacks the simple qualification of salesmanship, that he tends to talk at people instead of thinking with them.

6. Finally, many express the feeling that there is too much emphasis on *what* and too little on *how*. Many sermons are a sales talk for ends of thinking rather than a guide for creative thinking. They are likely to declare a faith but overlook reasons for the faith. They tell people what to believe without telling them how to come to a vital faith. They describe the world we should have, the persons we should be, the institutions we should fashion, the causes we should foster, but they are weak on suggesting how to do it, where to get the power, and how to win the skill.

II

What principles underlie preaching in the True Church? Let us look at the positive ways to make preaching vital.

1. The message must bear the mark of timeliness. Lynn Harold Hough, speaking before the students at Union Theological Seminary in New York, said, "The preacher must belong to his age. He needs to understand its passwords. He must be the master of its vocabulary. He must speak in a language that has meaning to his contemporaries." The minister of the True Church is in tune with his own age and with the moods of the hour. He starts where people are and leads them toward the fulfillment of God's will for their lives.

But preaching must also be timeless. The preacher cannot change as the contemporary climate changes. The pulpit cannot become a mirror in which men and women see reflected their favorite ideas and prejudices. In such a case the time comes when each influential layman expects to see his own face looking down at him from the pulpit. The minister must speak within the life of his age but above it. He must understand the mind and heart of his people, at the same time remembering that only that which is above the human enables men to keep their humanity. It is his task to lead men to find, to love, and to live by the will of God, and to grow from self into a sense of their common humanity.

2. The most important function of the sermon is to guide spiritual growth, linking up its message with the problems of everyday living. If the minister shares with his people in the various activities of the week, if he is close to the life of his children, young people, and adult men and women, his words will serve as an inspiration to spiritual growth. If, on the other hand, he is close only to books and volumes of sermons and magazines for preachers, and if he comes into his pulpit, centered only in abstract theology and doctrine, he denies the first principles of Christian fellowship.

If the sermon is to guide the spiritual growth of the worshiper, its emphasis should be on helping the congregation to share creatively in a thought process. It is easy to point out what is wrong in some particular situation, but far more difficult to guide people toward a decision for corrective action. It is simple to tell a person what to believe but more difficult to guide him in formulating reasons for his own faith. It is easier to talk about God than to lead people to know God. It is not difficult to preach a sermon that people forget—let any minister, two hours after he preaches, give his people an examination on the content of his sermon! In some churches printed or mimeographed copies of the sermon are available for personal study. In them may be recommended books that bear on the topic of the sermon. Oftentimes the sermon itself may be a part of an ongoing study program in the group life of the church, so that it either climaxes or serves as source material for further study.

A sermon ought to achieve with the worshiper the same relationship achieved in personal conference. In the sermon the minister describes some interest, some concern, or some field of thinking which he and his listeners will think about together. It may be a declaration of faith; it may be a sermon about God, Christ or prayer. It may concern the Church, the family, the child or the world community. The minister may bring an interpretive message about kinship with other nations. Or he may offer a character study of one of the great figures of the Bible, describing his problems, his objectives and failures, his weaknesses and strengths, how he won union with God or failed to win it, and finally showing the application of the discussion to contemporary living. Such a sermon on Job, for example, should make clear Job's unique contribution to an understanding of the nature of God. Sermons on the Ten Commandments, the Beatitudes, the Sermon on the Mount, or on Paul's letters, or the message of the prophets can be made experience-centered, if their application to present-day life is demonstrated.

On the other hand, there is the sermon that deals with fundamental personal problems—problems the individual faces in relation to his own life, to the lives of others and to the world. There is no doubt but that there should be sermons dealing with such specific problems, of which there are unlimited illustrations from everyday life. An employer, finding it necessary to remonstrate with an employee who makes mistakes in his work, considers which of three methods to employ: to rebuke him in the presence of all employees; to condemn him privately; or to ask him if there is any reason for his mistakes and offer understanding and help. A sermon on how to give criticism might take as its illustration the approach of the prophet to David, when the latter committed his sin. If the minister lives close to his people, he will be constantly confronted by the specific problems they face as individuals.

I was once asked, "Why not preach sometime on the subject, 'Why does not God prosper those who are faithful to Him?' " The inquirer went on to say that he had tried to live by the will of God, to follow the Ten Commandments and the teachings of Christ, but that he had had one experience of bad luck after another and, at that moment, was next to poverty. He pointed out the individuals who break all the rules, who profess one thing and do another, and who still prosper. The minister promised to preach on the problem as soon as he felt he had a God-given answer. He kept his promise, and found that the message had church-wide appeal.

When a specific problem is used as the basis for a sermon,

the message should follow lines of individual thinking. In a sermon on how to make prayer vital, these questions might be suggestive: Do you pray? When? What stands in the way of vital prayer? What are the intellectual difficulties? To whom do we pray? For whom or for what? How do we pray? What resources will help? Will we find help in the experiences of others who have found prayer vital? The sermon should face these problems, analyze them, offer ways to a solution and make clear the spiritual resources.

The sermon should be fundamentally directed at guiding the individual, and at helping him to face problems of the community, of the nation, and of the world. It does not merely state the problem and talk around it, but it helps to demonstrate specific steps by which the problems can be solved. The sermon will fall short unless it helps people in all walks of life to build collective relationships in harmony with the will of God. All of the concerns of the community, nation and world should be brought into the pulpit and given illumination and interpretation in the light of His will.

Certainly the sermon should also enlist people to the Christian life, pointing out the steps in becoming a true follower of the way. What are the follower's resources? How do people differ in their experience of God? How can one keep growing? These are all questions vital to the ministry of preaching.

One minister has a sermon committee of men and women who read his sermons before they are used. The members come together on a Saturday evening, having previously received a copy of the sermon for study. For the minister, it is an illuminating experience; for the committee members, a valued opportunity for useful participation. They check him on unclear language, at the same time giving an interest check as to the sermon's application to community life. If they question data, they ask the minister to review his authority. The members are representative of various political philosophies, of different occupations and economic levels, of diverse backgrounds. They keep him aware of the differing points of view and current attitudes in his congregation, and are especially helpful when the sermon deals with controversial matters. The minister has learned that if he is aware of the points of view of others, they are more ready to permit him freedom to preach the whole truth, in so far as it is revealed to him, in a spirit of love.

3. Sermons should be positive. Too many sermons are against everything. They are against evil instead of being for good, setting people in conflict with evil behavior rather than leading them to good ways of living. So much time is spent in describing evil that attention becomes centered on it rather than on its remedy.

The most constructive use for spiritual energy is to put it to work for positive goals. No alcoholic has ever found freedom simply by reminding himself that drinking is a bad habit. No one has ever furthered peace only by reiterating to himself the evils of war. Too much negative preaching inevitably encourages people to use their energy to fight that which they do not want, rather than to work for that in which they do believe. In a sense, this type of preaching "passes the buck" to God. It does not necessarily imply an advocacy of humanism for it accepts the fact that without God, man is helpless. But it does not make clear that God, without man's intent, is helpless to fulfill His plan.

There are preachers who lack in their own personalities the positive qualities of radiance, compassion, hopefulness, humor and courage. Often they are obstructed within by wrong thoughts of self, by fears and anxieties. They may have wrong concepts of religion and life, or their attitude toward life may be so unreal that they seem stuffy. It is possible for such an attitude to become an invisible barrier between the minister and his congregation. The true minister lets his love of God flow through him and out to his people. He loves truth and life; he is filled with the love and the radiance of the Divine.

4. Sermons are most meaningful when they grow out of the ongoing work of the beloved community and when they lead into individual and group action. In one church, the young people and adults center their attention on some one field, selecting from such subjects as prayer, what we expect of our schools, getting along with Russia, living as brothers with other races. The sermon introduces the topic on the first Sunday of the month. At the end of the month, another sermon draws together the findings of the study groups, reports progress, suggests ways of individual and collective action.

In another church a commission on social action compiles and interprets information and releases it with suggestions for action. When this commission recently prepared a report on "Peace with Russia without Appeasement," the minister preached a sermon on the subject, and copies of both his sermon and the commission report were made available to the congregation at the close of the service. The minister should be sensitive to the ongoing work of all of his church groups.

Pastors of some churches are proving themselves to be wholesomely receptive to the currents of thought among their members. When one of the younger members of one church asked, "What do we mean by our democracy?" the minister soon after preached a sermon on the subject, "Do We Believe in our Way of Life?" In another church where a youth group was studying comparative religions, the minister preached on the history and position of the Protestant, at the group's request. In still another group, parents were discussing how to put children to bed. When he heard of the interest in the subject, the minister preached a sermon on "Are Your Children Orphaned?"—a message on ways to a vital family fellowship.

One minister I know invites several study groups to help him think through problems. When he decided to preach a sermon on "Why Not Choose Health?" he asked physicians, dentists and psychiatrists in the church membership to plan the sermon with him. In another church there is a dinner meeting at which the sermon of the previous Sunday is discussed and methods of action are developed. Conclusions are printed in the church paper. One minister sends out a questionnaire to all his membership once every two years. He asks such questions as these: Are the sermons helpful and interesting to you? Name the three sermons that helped you most. What individual concerns would you like discussed in sermons? What social problems? What recommendations do you have for the sermons and the worship service? What suggestions do you have regarding the work of our church?

If sermons grow out of individual, community and world needs, they are bound to have more value. If they lead to action, they have fulfilled their true purpose.

5. A fundamental principle of preaching is that it must interpret faith to this generation and show its relationship to reason.

Faith is the brave hypothesis of which life is the brave experiment. Faith is passionate intuition, an undying fire in the soul of man. Faith is never opposed to reason, except when it ceases to be a faith and becomes a form of superstition. The scientist lives by his faith that the sky is trustworthy. The explorer reaches his Pillars of Hercules, and in faith cries, "More beyond!" The research doctor has faith that a cure can be found for a dread disease. In the nature of things, he cannot offer any logical assurance that a cure can be found—he works by faith. But his faith is not the foe of his reason. His faith is reason grown full of courage.

To say that life is only dust reduces the human race to a level of insanity. To say that there is no discernible meaning to life is to leave us, as George Buttrick says, chewing our finger tips for sustenance. Learning, consciously or unconsciously, lives by faith. Religion offers a faith not only for knowledge but for the whole of life and death. The Christian faith avows that what is highest in spirit is deepest in nature.

The minister must make clear the relationship between knowledge and reverence. Reverence has always been suspicious of learning, mainly on the ground that learning too easily becomes haughty and loveless. Did not Jesus say that God had "hid these things from the wise and the prudent and hast revealed them unto babes"? On the other hand, learning often distrusts religion. For, as Alfred North Whitehead has said, almost scathingly, religion has been more eager to defend partial truth than to seek fuller truth. The struggle of the Church against new truth is well known. Too often the Church is the victim of yesterday.

Thus there is a conflict between truth and religion. Galileo proposed, as many do in our day, that the two realms should stand forever separate; religion for Sunday, science for Monday. Unfortunately, the same man lives through Sunday and Monday, and no one has yet succeeded in dividing man's personality into secular and sacred compartments. The self who prays and seeks to weave the insights of prayer into everyday life is the same as the self who thinks. Religion should quicken knowledge. Someone described God as "what happens to me when I see homing birds against a sunset sky," but that same emotional experience can purvey knowledge of birds and of refraction of light. Conversely, knowledge should quicken reverence. Kepler, overcome by the majesty of the stars, felt that he was thinking God's thoughts after him. We cannot separate learning from religion, and it is the preacher and teacher's job to find the true relationship between them.

The minister must also help the individual find reason for faith in God, in a purposeful universe, in man, in Christian fellowship. There are basic and logical reasons back of faith in God, reasons which have an academic acceptability in these days. When one looks at the patternfulness of the universe, it is inconceivable to think that life came into being accidentally. E. Stanley Jones loves to say, "How often would you have to throw up a handful of type for it to fall down in the pattern of a Shakespearean play?" The fact that there is in life the quality of the personal indicates that there must be, in the universe, that which is personal. For how could the impersonal create the personal? The fact that man has the capacity for kinship and fellowship leads us to believe that there is a like capacity at the heart of the universe. Nothing cannot create something! And the fact that man sooner or later seeks God is evidence that there must be a searching heart at the core of living, a heart that ever seeks the best in men.

III

What is the message of preaching in the True Church?

The sermon sets forth the glory of God in conscious intelligence and moral love, eternally alive. It interprets the life of man, a being of critical capacity whose intelligence demonstrates itself in the exercise of that which makes him a man, namely, the freedom to choose. It deals with the tragedies, the remorses and the bondages of humanity which has used its freedom in such a way as to lose it and to betray its own destiny. Its concern is to keep alive in man's soul the love and longing, the power and peace, that follow from unity with God.

The sermon interprets the life, the teachings and the spirit of Christ in whom God became fully incarnate. It deals with the love and goodness and redeeming power of God through whom the human soul attains eternal life. It describes the great acceptances through which man enters into the loving fellowship of the forgiven; and the great rejections which make of man's soul a battleground of violent forces. It has to do with moral judgments and consequences of denying or ignoring God. It has to do with forces of potential evil which, by God's grace, can be bent to His purpose. It is concerned with all the resources that bring about the coming of the Kingdom in the soul of the individual and of humanity. It explains the immortality of the soul. It draws upon all those timeless elements of religion that speak to all ages with an ageless power.

The sermon deals both with the individual and with society, those two which are, as George Buttrick has said, terms of a single paradox.

The seat of all things human is selfhood. Personality is the pole around which the electrons of the social life revolve. Granted that we are bound in a bundle of life more closely than leaves are bound in the life of a tree—each leaf is yet different and distinct. If mankind is a stupendous organism, personalities are yet its life-giving cells. The individual is still the fount and nexus of our social life.[2]

[2] *Jesus Came Preaching*, by George Buttrick (New York: Charles Scribner's Sons, 1931), p. 82.

If this basic fact is forgotten, the preacher will find himself speaking of movements and of causes as if they were not animated by people. He must remember that if human solidarity is to be proclaimed, humanity must proclaim it. And before humanity can proclaim it, one mind must envision it and envision it alone in worship. "The spirit of the Lord came upon Gideon," says the old story. Literally, the words are: "The spirit of the Lord clothed himself with Gideon." Literally, the eternal invaded society through a chosen personality. Every crusade has as its spear point a consecrated spirit. Every cause and movement must finally come as a supplicant to an individual altar.

To make more specific the message of the sermon, the minister of the True Church approaches each problem from the viewpoint of the individual. In all of Jesus' teachings and in his Sermon on the Mount, it is very clear that he was speaking to the individual. In the first chapter we pointed out that he was interested in the coming of the Kingdom within each individual soul. "All Heaven rejoices over one sinner that is saved."

Humanity is crying and dying for a new definition of man. Misinterpretation of the Darwinian hypothesis has robbed man of his sense of destiny, and his impoverishment is expressing itself in his tastes, his morals and his citizenship. There is no question but that the concepts of individual freedom and of political self-government rise out of Jesus' strange and revolutionary teaching that man is a priceless, immortal being, and that the total purpose and intent of society is to free man's imprisoned splendor in order that he may fulfill his destiny as a son of God.

Christianity is a faith in life. It teaches immortality because it believes that the majesty of life comes from and returns to God. The whole power of Christianity rests on its faith that the

Eternal God, just as He became a humble carpenter and lived in grace and beauty among men, will also live in us if we surrender to Him. Therein is the sublime exaltation of the possibilities of the human spirit.

It is a world-changing doctrine. And wherever it has gone it has struck shackles from slaves, it has made men discontented with ignorance and narrowness, and especially has it beaten against the barred gates of cruelty and injustice. Its progress has not been steady. Men have turned to easier faiths and more comfortable creeds, but wherever this vital religion has taken root, there has followed the enrichment and release of man.

It is to this high purpose and with this great conviction that the preacher proclaims the will of God for the individual soul in all its relations. The sermon, first of all, is concerned with the individual soul and its relationship with God. Here the soul meets its highest conflict. The brook, Jabbok, where Jacob wrestled with the angel, is not only a Palestinian stream but a current that runs by every human life. No soul quite escapes the yearning appeal of God. The remorse that stabs awake, that is God. The strange, impossible ideal that beckons and lures, that is God. The glory of faithful love, that is God. The desire in us for the best, that always is God.

The sermon in the True Church constantly helps the individual in his search to discover the meaning of life and the purpose of the universe. The sermon speaks of God and His nature, of His purpose and the forms of His revelation. It sets forth the meaning of prayer and shows how prayer may become vital in personal and in corporate worship. It interprets the insights and contribution of Jesus, and the vision and methods of all the saints who, finding the way to God, made the way plain to others. It explains the basis of belief in immortality and its vital significance to life.

In the second place, the sermon is concerned with the relation of the individual soul to its environment. Every individual is in constant conflict with influences about him. It may be conflict resulting from illness, from defeated ambition, from unrequited love, or the conflict of the sensitive soul, rearing and charging against the injustices and cruelties of the world.

The minister who is close to his people and sensitive to their needs will see them as they are, a procession of frustrated human beings. But for him the question that arises out of all human experience will not be whether man must meet frustration, but what he does under its pressures. The Cross is an eternal witness of the triumph that can lead out of frustration. There is so much in life that denies faith in God, so much that seems a ruthless march of vast indifference, that faith must again and again call upon all its reserves to fend off deadly despair. Who has not heard this cry of the tortured soul as expressed by Jean Paul Richter:

I have traveled the world. I have risen to the sun. I have passed athwart the great waste spaces of the sky. I have discovered the place where the very shadow of being dies out and ends. I have gazed into the gulf and cried, "Father, where art Thou?" But no answer came save the sound of the eternal storm that rages uncontrolled. We are orphans, you and I.

But this is only one reading of the facts. The sermon must make clear that there is another interpretation, formed by men who have known life just as fully and have found it just as difficult and as bewildering. In the very consecration of their suffering, men of faith have found strength and confidence. The sermon makes clear that the problem of good is just as inexplicable as the problem of evil. For several years there comes a drought that sears the land, and fields that once turned from green to gold with fruitful harvest now lie parched and barren. "What kind of God is it who sends such a plague?" we ask. But did anyone during all the years of bountiful harvest cry, "O God, the goodness of Thy bounty and the mystery of Thy generosity is past our understanding!" Why is it that we think that beauty and blessing are normal to life, but that disappointment and tragedy are ruthless intruders? Why, in the same world where there is the ageless wickedness of war, is there also the unfailing love of mothers? If there is the devastating hurricane, there is also the gentle splendor of the summer's setting sun.

It is not only the evil of the world that baffles our minds, but its glory as well. If I say, "I will not longer struggle with the problem of suffering, rather will I give up my belief in God," then I am left to account for all the goodness and heroism, the hopes and dreams and sacrifices of men, as well as the beauty with which the artist has filled the world. But if I choose the God and Father of our Lord Jesus and determine to trust Him, the world's creator and redeemer, then I am left to wrestle with the world's pain.

To an honest mind, unbelief cannot be an escape from mystery. In human experience there are the bases for desolating doubts, as well as for creative and adventurous belief. Christian faith is that high resolution of will that determines to live by the soul's highest affirmation, its unalterable conviction. Life is made up of black and white squares, but, as Phillips Brooks used to say, "the central belief of the Christian is that the black squares are against the white background"—that the dark mystery of the world's evil is a patchwork pattern against the radiant mystery of the world's good.

We can see the relation of evil and good in another light. When we are sick, the resources of the great human family come to our rescue. When we eat, when we dress, when we communicate, when we ride, we are the beneficiaries of the efforts of the universal human family. Shall we, then, receiving untold benefits from our membership in the family, deem it unfair when we are asked to bear the consequences of family ignorance, family folly, and family sin? We can only have the benefits if we accept the risks.

Life is never static. It is a comedy to one who thinks and a tragedy to one who feels. Life is pain and disappointment and loneliness. It is burden and battle and anguish; ignorance and blunder and defeat. Life is love bereaved; ideals never achieved; gladness soon becoming grief; morning fading quickly into night. Life is a vast wilderness; it is a perennial mystery.

Religion at its best never denies confusion and suffering. Jesus faced the whole tragedy that is at the heart of life, and plunged into the deepest darkness of the world's pain. All the desperate tides of the world's woe coursed through the channels of this soul. Religion is no release from tragedy. It is a faith big enough to include tragedy. It is not an escape from darkness but an enduring confidence in the midnight.

In the religion of Jesus, the Cross and the Crown are two inseparable symbols. Jesus won his Crown through embracing the Cross, through suffering; through absorbing into his own love the guilt and sins of the world, through lifting up his pain as a precious offering unto God. Jesus went through the night into the eternal morning. He knew sin as no one has ever known it. He laid his breast against the world's woeful heart, to hear its agonizing beat and to feel all its throbbing hurt. But Jesus said sin and pain were not the ultimates of life. Death and destiny are not synonymous. The shame of sin, the soul's sorrow—these are temporary frustrations. They do not alter the direction of life's onward sweep. The positive, all-conquering forces in human experience are goodness and truth. In every generation there have been those who have found the secret by which they have overcome self, who have found in their suffering the elements of victory. For them, defeat and loss became a stair, sloping upward through the darkness to God. It is not the circumstances of life that break or uplift us, but our misinterpretation of them. That is a matter of the soul. The soul that fights for its imperial right to believe will find data for belief, even in life's darkest moment. The soul can make the circumstances serve it. The soul can make its own climate and create its own environment.

The sermon is ever concerned to help the soul in its effort to right the wickedness and wrongs of the world. No one who himself knows the love and peace of happy home life can be content unless he helps others find it. No one can have a sense of security without helping to bring it to others. No one with peace in his heart can be satisfied unless he gives the best he has to the building of a peaceful community, nation and world. No one can basically believe in honesty without doing everything in his power to help people discover those principles of living which make honesty possible within and without their lives. In the admonishing words of James, "Be ye doers of the word, and not hearers only."

Consequently, in its larger aspects, the sermon is always interested in the individual's relationship to social groups and to society as a whole. It is concerned with social injustice, unemployment, the exploitation of human personality for personal gain. It evaluates all institutions from the standpoint of their effect on human personality.

The sermon deals with the relationship of the individual to the church, and with the responsibility of the Church to the individual. The sermon strives for a breadth of social vision that helps the individual to make his fullest contribution to the community and to society. The pulpit is interested in the problems of Christian citizenship and in its opportunities, in the relation of religion to politics and in the role of the individual Christian in government. The pulpit is deeply concerned with the larger frustrations among nations, with the clash of different nationalisms and with the role of individual and collective groups of Christians in working for international peace.

With reference to the individual and his environment, a very specific field of the sermon is the relationship of the individual to his family. The sermon is concerned with the purpose and function of the family and with its place in God's plan. It prepares the individual for Christian family life. The sermon makes a contribution to the relationships of husband and wife, and of parents to children and children to parents. It helps to establish and make vital the altar of worship in the home. It makes clear the way to rich family life and encourages family members to share in its enrichment. The sermon motivates families to help one another.

The sermon is vitally concerned with the individual's relationship to the larger family of which he is a part—the nation. It helps him to envision, to understand and to consecrate himself to the democratic ideals of our Republic. By guiding the individual to more Christian attitudes, it seeks to make ours a more Christian nation.

Politically speaking, democracy as conceived in America rests upon the sovereignty of the individual and makes its political decisions on the basis of the uncoerced and unhampered vote of the majority. It is predicated on the Christian belief in the sacredness of man. Just as Christianity asks of man that he surrender self to the will of God, democracy asks of the citizen that he surrender selfish interests to the good of the nation. It recognizes individual differences and seeks to develop each person's abilities. It has faith in man and in man's ability to choose. While it functions by the vote of the majority, it protects the right of the minority, recognizing that with change and progress the minority may, in time, become the majority. Democracy believes in equality before the law, and is committed to equal opportunity for all men. It does not profess to be perfect, but inherent in the democratic system is the mechanism for correcting its imperfections and mistakes. And in that single characteristic lie the possibilities that make of democracy a dangerous and a thrilling experiment—dangerous, because it has the freedom to destroy itself; and thrilling, because it can, with time, make the will of government synonymous with the will of God.

"The difficulty for a democracy is," wrote Matthew Arnold, "how to find and keep high ideals. The individuals who compose it are, the bulk of them, persons who need to follow an ideal, not to set one. . . .[3] Therein lies the responsibility of the minister, the message of the sermon, the role of the Church itself, as they concern man and his government. From God come the ideals for social living and the courage to maintain them. They do not come effortlessly. They are born in the individual's

[3] *The Popular Education of France*, by Matthew Arnold, in *Harper's Anthology: Prose* (New York: Harper & Brothers, 1926), p. 409.

painstaking search of his own soul for the will of God. They are strengthened as he learns to live within his own family, to fit himself into a group, to recognize needs other than his own. They reach their highest expression in a government to which each individual brings all the product of his efforts, in a government built on the Christian principles of freedom, participation and brotherhood.

The sermon must not overlook discussion of the history of the Church and its significance. At the same time that it points out the differences between the three branches of the Christian Church—the Eastern Orthodox, the Roman Catholic and the Protestant—it shows their basic unity. The sermon is never interested in setting one worshiper against another, but in helping the individual to discover God's purpose for *any* Church; or, indeed, for any institution dedicated to furthering a just and decent way of life. Out of the scriptures and other holy writings, the sermon draws data to reconstruct the historical background of the True Church. It helps the individual to understand the significance of the man-made additions to the institution that is the modern Church. It interprets the Church in its true light, as based upon a universal priesthood of all believers. It makes clear that the meaning and purpose undergirding the True Church rest upon authority in the Bible and all the holy writings in which God's will is revealed.

The pulpit is concerned, in the third place, with the soul's struggle within itself. However good and evil came into the world, they are strangely mixed in the soul of man. An ancient poet sings, "God took the dust of the earth and made man and he became a living soul." Certainly both dust and divinity are there: slothfulness which could make comfortable dwelling in the muck of life's swampy lowlands, and winged desire that would find its home amid the silvery silence of the stars. Of such is man, no less lured by good than tempted by evil; as often earth-bound as heaven-inspired.

The sermon makes clear that the struggle is won only by discipline. It makes clear that temptation alone makes sin, that it is only the possibility of higher good that allows any place for evil. Sin is the refusal to grow. The heart is not evil, and the man who lives on the level of the heart is not evil, except when he refuses to realize the deepest potentiality of his spirit as well. He is not evil unless he refuses to grow in the nature and mind and life of God. What the individual might be forever calls out to what he is. It is some divine discontent mingled with all his joy that keeps man struggling, forever a pilgrim on the earth.

The minister of the True Church knows the conflicts men face in the hidden places of the soul, the wars that are waged with temptation. He knows the doubts that must be stifled, the hungers that must be disciplined, the disappointments that must be met, the selfishness that must be put aside.

In every soul there is a grasping, acquisitive self. It is so much apparent and so often dominant that some say it is all there is in man. They say that the only hope of the world's progress is in the enlightenment of man's selfishness. There is, they say, no appeal that can be made to man save on the basis of this outreaching egotism. But that is not true. Life might be simpler and more understandable if it were true. But in the heart of man is not only self regard, but also a deep, hidden regard for others. Altruism is also a part of human nature. Its voice may be stifled, its modest flowers may be trampled under the feet of a flinty wordliness, but it is there. It expresses itself in every small act of human helpfulness. It finds its crown in a parent's love. Beside the factory where women and men are exploited without just compensation, there rises the public library, built by philanthropy in order that all may read. Here are industrial conditions that impair health, and there is the hospital where the sick may freely find the best of medical care and skill.

That is why we see compassion for the poor becoming the bandwagon upon which men ride to political preferment. That is why in some men we see the puzzling paradox of sincere service to mankind blemished by the greedy gathering of selfish emoluments. There are the tensions and the conflicts. There is not a soul who does not know that battle. The truth about man has not been better told than in Plato's great figure of a charioteer driving two steeds. One is vibrant with spiritual beauty, the other strong in sensual energy. It is the task of the charioteer to bring his two horses to pull as a team.

There is always the strife between comfortable illusion and disturbing truth. The actual never gets away from the claim of the ideal. The struggle goes on, its harvest either to become the bulwark of a finer civilization, or to fall into the melancholy ruins of a society crumbling to a dreamless dust. But greater than the fact of struggle is the fact of God's help on the side of the soul who strives to transcend self and to follow the highest truth. To the Christian weary with the hard-fought battle, the sound of His voice and the touch of His hand are the supremest joy the soul can know.

IV

Each minister is called upon to set up many pulpits beyond the sanctuary. There is the pulpit of the radio and of the public platform and the small group. There is the message of the preacher at the service of memory. There is the minister's opportunity to guide one of the most significant worship experiences in the life of the individual—the marriage ceremony. These experiences of worship "beyond the pulpit" many times reach individuals who do not come to church, and provide the minister with invaluable opportunities to enlist people in the True Church. If he makes the right use of these opportunities, he may remove many of the stumbling blocks from their path to the Church, and may free many individuals from that which keeps them from active church participation. The obstacle may be indifference, it may be fear or resentment. The opportunities presented and the seeds sown in these experiences beyond the pulpit may have unlimited possibilities.

Let us look briefly at these additional pulpits, both outside of the sanctuary and within it, which the minister of the True Church uses with wisdom and with effectiveness.

Whether the minister speaks over the radio or from the public platform, whether to a large group or small, his message has certain basic characteristics in common with the sermon. His message, like that of the sermon, centers in life, dealing with the one of its aspects that is most vital to his audience. It is alive and warm in tone. It should, if possible, point to specific action.

No matter when or where the speech is given, it makes clear that all men are spiritual and that the purpose of life is to develop their spiritual nature. If that point is not made clear, the minister does not speak as a true minister, and the group to which he speaks might better listen to a lay or technical authority in the field. For in the secular world in which we live, men hear little enough outside the Church about God and His purpose. Only in the church building do they learn about human personality and its divine destiny, about the great spiritual resources of life, about the principles of human living as laid down by Jesus and by all those others who found the will of God. Wherever he speaks, the minister ought to make sure that somehow, in some way, his message bears upon the faith to which he is devoted.

Once I heard Robert Norwood give a twelve-minute message to a group of teachers at Columbia University. His topic was "Enemies." He started out simply and to the point, stating that he had three things to say about enemies. The first was that the worst enemy is a friend gone wrong. He spoke for a few minutes about the tragedy of broken friendships, and with skill touched on the whole cycle of them, from the tiffs of school children to the breaches among nations.

His second point was that an enemy does himself the most harm. He elaborated on it with skill, making application of the danger of secret criticism among teachers or leaders. No man is great enough, he pointed out, to lead one to hate him.

At the end he concluded his whole speech with his third simple point: an admonition never to be any man's enemy.

It was a perfect sermon, given in the spirit of an intimate talk. Without the use of the words "God" or "Christ" or "prayer," there was yet achieved the quality of worship. Although it was not preaching, it was a sermon in the finest sense.

There are times, before professional groups, when the minister speaks with intellectual depth. He is able to bring to such messages the full meaning of the Church and of religion. He understands and interprets the contribution of all the sciences and arts to religion. He is conversant with current books and illumined on world issues so that, through him, the True Church keeps abreast of contemporary thought.

The minister of the True Church regards the funeral service not only as commemorative, but as a service of worship in its truest sense. The service of memory can suggest something of the unlimited possibilities of human love when God is in the hearts of those who share it. It reminds that, in spite of death, the individual soul continues to fulfill God's purpose for life through those he loves and those who loved him. The service of memory should, in the True Church, free those who are bereaved from being anchored to the moment's grief and to the earthly tomb. It gives them strength to grow and to live by the faith and hope and triumph which death cannot deny them.

The marriage ceremony in the True Church is a worship service of the highest order. Next to the individual's commitment to God and His will through Christ, no sacrament is more significant than the service in which two people accept the vows of marriage. Because of its sanctity, the service is most fittingly performed in the sanctuary. If the True Church has served a vital and real purpose in the lives of its young people, they will want their marriage consecrated in its sanctuary. It is important that they can have their wedding there without too great cost. The wedding ceremony that is a costly social event has little relation to a service dedicated to the exchange of vows before God.

V

Other media for the sermon are available to the minister of the True Church. There is the message of the printed page, the message of pictures and drama and music.

The pulpit of the printed page is used effectively in the True Church. Each unit of the Church should have pamphlets, magazines, publications and books that bear on the purpose of growth in spiritual life, individually and corporately. It makes available to its members informative literature on the world activities of the Church and on the concerns of the human family in its local, national and world relations. The True Church seeks by every method to convey its message, to help people to think and to grow in mind and in spirit and in soul.

There is the message that can be portrayed in pictures. There are many movies of great value. There are illustrated lectures that concern the Bible, the history of the Church, right forms of human behavior, the activities of the universal Church. Wherever the minister can use slides and movies to advantage in presenting the message of religion, it should be done. The True Church building has equipment with which the fullest use can be made of visual aids and movies. They should be included in programs for the whole congregation, as well as in those for smaller study groups.

There is the message of drama. Within each unit of the True Church there ought to be a dramatic group. The reader will remember reference in an earlier chapter to a church which has a director of the theater on its staff. Great religious, moral and ethical plays are presented, to which church members and residents of the community can come free of charge. It has been observed that the power and effectiveness of this theater has almost equaled the power of the pulpit in the morning worship service, in conveying the message of the Church. Dramatic groups serve a double purpose in the Church program. Those who take part learn new values of participation and grow in appreciations they might not learn elsewhere. For those who witness, the inspirational appeal is even more compelling to thought and growth of the spirit.

There is also the ministry of music in the True Church. Some units of the Church have vesper services in the afternoon which are largely musical, offering participation to choral groups of children, young people and adults. The great messages of religion—the vision and purpose and majesty of God, the victory of Christ, the glory of the human soul, the cleansing of the spirit—are given magnificent expression through oratorios, anthems, hymns and other forms of sacred music. The minister of the True Church uses choirs and glee clubs of all ages to serve as another pulpit through which to reach the individual and to add beauty to the experience of corporate worship.

All preaching in the True Church culminates in the hope that individual church members will themselves become preachers, to carry forth the message of the Church and to win others to the way of God. The pulpit is most vital when it enlists its laymen in the preaching of the Church. Strictly professional preaching, indeed, may always be bad. But the corrective of bad preaching lies not, as the glib critics of the day gleefully proclaim, in the cessation of preaching: the remedy lies in good preaching. As an incentive to this end I have offered my suggestions.

VII ∾∾∾

IT DEMANDS NEW LEADERSHIP

THE True Church calls for leaders who are themselves free to grow in the will of God and in making His will manifest to others. It calls for leaders who have progressed from self-centeredness to an increasing awareness of God and to a deep consciousness of their oneness with all humanity. Its very life and growth depends on leaders whose wholehearted passion is to help others rise above the level of materialism, to grow in the life of the spirit, and to participate in the building of the beloved community.

There is urgency and haste in the cry of the True Church for new strength. If the future's children are to be conceived in a world with any slight promise of peace, the old crumbling foundations of society must be replaced by new groundworks. And their construction must begin now. The chance of yesterday is already gone, and tomorrow's opportunity will be too late. The work must begin today. It must begin today in my thinking and in your thinking, in my heart and in your heart. In the slow, arduous process of rebuilding, only fragments of the new walls will rise in the years left to us, but our children may yet live in the beloved communities of a world marked by security, decency and honor to God.

Wherever there is a unit of the True Church led by a true minister, there the process of rebuilding has already begun. There justice, righteousness and mercy are taking root in the community. There spirituality flourishes. There love of God and men increases, and the evidences of God's grace become increasingly clear. The numbers of the True Church are as yet small. Its test lies not in its numbers but in the sincere quality of living among those who belong to its fellowship.

To consider the skill and resources that went into discovering the secret of atomic energy is to understand how such an achievement was made possible. The best scientific minds were enlisted. Money was spent without stint. Perhaps never before in history had there been such total consecration of brain and heart and leadership and money to achieve any goal. And if there is to be the wisdom in the world to use this energy for human good rather than human destruction, it can only come with consecration of the individual to live by the will of God and to act in harmony with the moral order of the universe.

There are those who feel that humanity hovers on the immediate brink of extinction. But whether or not this is true, whether or not it is a matter of continuing life or immediate death for our culture, there must arise the vision, the purpose and the will within individuals and nations to use the resources that science has made available for the good of all men. In this process it is the Church in all its strength—the *True* Church— that must lead men to discover the God-mind for this generation. It is the Church that must lead them to discover those goals which are worthy of the supreme devotion of all men, and which, if achieved, will at last mean liberty and peace and justice for all.

For the Church to accomplish this high purpose, new leadership must be enlisted and trained. The minister is the key to the growth of the Church. He must be its preacher and pastor. He must direct its finances and guide its educational work. He is responsible for relations between the Church and the public;

he represents the Church in community functions. In many churches he does most of the work, except teaching the classes in the Sunday school. He must have the qualities of a salesman to enable him to be close to his people. He must have some administrative ability. If he is effective, the Church reaches out to people and is looked upon as a success. An ineffective minister inevitably results in an ineffective Church.

We have already pointed out the ineffectiveness of much preaching and ministerial leadership, and the inadequacies of seminary training. The contemporary Church itself is inadequate for many reasons. Thirty per cent of all local churches are not able to support a full-time minister. It is estimated that only 30 per cent more can support a minister, a part-time secretary, and a janitor. Only 5 per cent of the Protestant churches in America have adequate staffs to guide an all-round ministry and, at the same time, direct a comprehensive training program for lay leadership.

In the face of these inadequacies in the system of Protestant denominationalism, the True Church seeks four practicable goals. The first is to combine local churches wherever possible, in order to make them large enough to support an adequate professional staff, to build the beloved community and to provide for the full guidance of individual growth in spirit. The second is to enlist and train a strong quality of leadership for all aspects of the church ministry. Contingent on the acceptance of the first goal, this will only be possible when there are more churches capable of providing the opportunity and the resources for employing such leadership.

A third goal is to recruit and train specialized leadership for activities beyond the major function of preaching and pastoral work. Ideally, the True Church has a trained leader for each one of its many spheres of activity—for its preaching ministry, for its work with children, youth, the family and adults; for its ministry of music, of religious psychotherapy, of vocational guidance and for any other activities which it has resources to support. Obviously, no one man can adequately perform the functions of all of these. And equally obvious is the fact that such specialization is only possible in a large and well-established church institution. But not until the Church includes some or all of these ministers and ministries, will it fulfill its true purpose. Because we are not satisfied with a one-room school, headed by a teacher expected to teach all subjects, schools have been consolidated in order to provide leaders equipped to teach various ages and to give guidance in specialized areas. The True Church cherishes the same hope for itself and believes that it can, with time and planning, be achieved.

The fourth objective of the True Church is to enlist and consecrate lay leaders, guiding them to dedicate their natural abilities and to learn new skills so that they may share in all phases of the Church's ministry.

I

The True Church demands leadership that can begin with a situation typical of the contemporary Church as it now exists, and gradually lead the people of the community toward organizing one True Church as we have conceived it. Or, if the community is without a church, the effort of leadership should be directed toward leading the people to build one unit of the True Church in that community. If the Church can serve the same area as the school district, it is an ideal situation. If the building can be located close to a school building, it will be helpful.

If there are two or more churches in the same community, the first question is whether there are resources available to develop each separate church into an effective unit of the True Church. Unless there are such resources, there will be perpetuated a competitive situation that lessens the spiritual power of the Church as a whole and that divides the community rather than unites it. Lacking such resources, the need is for leadership that can bring these churches either to federate or to co-operate.

There are eight churches, for instance, in a town of eighteen hundred people. If each is a unit of the True Church, their ministers will work together. In the spirit of the True Church, they will make a job-analysis of the spiritual leadership available in the community. They will assign to each church the specific ministry or service which it is best fitted to undertake. Regular services may be held in each church and all ministers may preach, but beyond that there will be a co-operative program. One church may specialize in training workers with children; another in youth-work training, and another in training leaders for adults. One may center its work on counseling and on developing a program of mental hygiene for all the churches. One may work in the field of religious drama; another in the area of creative use of leisure. Another may build relations with the school, the social agencies and other organizations in the community. One may guide the training program in marriage and the family. Together they may employ a leader trained in emotional guidance and growth. In time, all together might employ a person trained in the field of religious music. The choirs from each church, united in a community choir, could serve as a powerful religious force in the community, ministering to community-wide activities.

By working together they become in spirit a single church. In time the vision will come for one united church for the eighteen hundred people of the community. With united resources, funds will be available for employing a staff of ministers adept in the various fields of the united church's ministry.

If one or more of the churches in such a community are reluctant to co-operate, then those who have committed themselves to participation should proceed. If only four out of eight churches unite and become vital and effective, with a comprehensive ministry and an outstanding staff of professional leaders, they will not only attract most of the people in the town, but they will become the community's regenerative force. They will attract the children and the young people, and through them, their parents.

It is a slow and laborious process to move from small, competitive units of the contemporary Church into a large, vital community of the True Church with resources adequate for leadership and ministering to community needs. It takes patience and prayer and diligence. It means willingness on the part of ministers to stay in the same community for a period of years. It means that seminaries must revise their curriculum so as to train ministers in a wide variety of skills, recognizing that some will be for a time in churches where they must perform all the leadership functions, while others will need specialized training in particular fields.

It also means growth in the life of the spirit on the part of the minister. He is no longer set apart as an individual man of God. Instead he becomes a part of a team for God. He works with others. He recognizes that he alone cannot do it. He sees that it is the job of a team and not of an individual. His motivation is not the adulation he receives but the spiritual growth that results within individual and community life.

In addition, it means that national denominational groups must find, as soon as possible, a way by which they may unite in guiding communities toward the achievement of local churches large enough for adequate leadership and resourceful enough for full ministry. In the national denominational boards, the True Church demands a quality of leadership that is free from the necessities of promoting an institution or of saving an organizational pattern. It demands leadership dedicated to the fullest growth of the individual spirit and consecrated to the support of whatever institutions best foster that growth.

II

The True Church calls for new leadership throughout the whole structure of Protestantism. On the state level it demands leadership with time and ability to supervise and give training to the local church. Many of the leaders now working in the state denominational and interdenominational organizations either have never had experience in the local church or were unsuccessful there. An unusually well-qualified leader is needed to direct training and provide supervision whereby leaders in local churches may grow in vision, understanding and in the ability to create their own materials as they work with their own people. The best training takes place in processes of demonstration.

Not only is there need for a new type of area supervisor and counselor, but there is desperate need for teamwork among those who are now functioning. Today, in most of the states in our country, the larger denominations have their own state organizations with one or more field workers. These field workers, for the most part, work independent of other denominations and other organizations. In a number of states there are, at the same time, state councils of churches, made up of the Protestant denominations and employing field workers. While the denominational and state council men theoretically work together, their programs are, in actuality, competitive.

A year ago I attended a state council convention in one of our richest states. Only one denominational field man was present at the convention, and he came from the national office. On inquiry, it was learned that, at the same time the denominations were sponsoring the convention through the co-operative state council organization, the leaders of the denominations were conducting meetings of their own that were in a real sense competitive.

The council of churches, which is the denominations in co-operation, is the logical center for all the field work activities in the state. This has been successfully achieved in New Jersey where each of the various denominations supplies a field worker for the state council and pays his salary. The result is that the New Jersey council, serving a small state, has a well-trained children's director, youth director and adult worker, as well as other specialized leadership for weekday schools of religion and vacation Bible schools. It has made possible a strong staff for the co-operative state organization and at the same time has been a step in the direction of a united field program. Since the programs of the various Protestant denominations are essentially the same, it is not only foolish but potentially sinful that they should not work together on a basis of unity.

One of the most hopeful opportunities for united action in the Church is the summer camp for youth. Where larger local units of the Church have been achieved, they have their own camps but, at best, this is not sufficient. The young people of one local unit of the Church should share with young people from other units. The same principle of sharing among local units of the Church should be followed throughout all activities of all age groups.

One of the most effective summer programs for youth in the nation has been under the supervision of the Pennsylvania Council of Christian Education. The council has an attractive camp site to which young people, people of college age and adult leaders come in the summer for training. There are young people from local churches and from county youth councils. There are adult leaders from local churches and from adult councils. Here they work together; here they get training not only in building the True Church in the local community but in building it in the larger areas of the county and state.

We need to provide opportunity for interpenetration of culture. We need to bring young people from the city to share with youth in the country; young people of laboring families to share with those whose parents are in business and professional fields. All branches of the Church, all nationalities and all races should share in the interchange of experience and idea.

If the Protestant denominations were to take seriously the councils of churches, they could have outstanding summer camp programs in states throughout the country. Here people of all ages could share together, receive training and see the vision of the True Church and discover ways to work for it. Here real spiritual growth could be achieved in the summer months. Here a sense of unity in the work of the Kingdom could develop and grow. More actual spiritual growth can be achieved in one week in camp than in a year's effort in the average contemporary Church.

The True Church calls for leadership that can bring unity to the state church organization. There are social issues that need to be tackled on a united basis, and political issues that need to be given nonpartisan emphasis. There are national and world concerns that the local church must bring to its altar. A unified approach to such problems on the part of the state council or federation can be of infinite value to the local units of the Church.

Religious use of radio time ought to be a part of both local and state-wide activities of the Church. The Maine Council of Churches has done remarkable work in providing Sunday schools for children and young people in areas where there are no churches. These are areas able to afford only one church, that must go without worship services because the denominational system has not developed a plan for any unified church. In the meantime, the churches of the state, working together through the Maine Council, provide for them the best equivalent through the use of radio. It is participation of significance and fine opportunity. The full possibilities of religious radio have not yet been adequately envisioned. Religious forums, talks on spiritual guidance, services for individual and family worship, the discussion, from a religious point of view, of the great concerns of the world—all these could be offered on a sound basis through a unified program for using radio facilities.

It is important that the Church have an opportunity to develop the best public relations through the press. In my own state, the Catholic church has achieved a state-wide publicity program through the press which is tremendously useful. The Catholics have the resources and leadership, the strategy and plan for it. It bears rich fruit. The Protestant branch of the Church should have similarly good public relations, not on a competitive basis but to fulfill its true mission. Such a campaign can only be carried out through unified action. It could be done by a strong, powerful and vigorous council of Protestant churches to which the separate denominations would surrender sovereignty and in which they would merge their staff so that all field work, supervision and program promotion is carried out on a united basis. The denominations will realize, when the spirit of the True Church is achieved, that in so doing they are not losing but are gaining in strength.

The True Church, in like manner, calls for new national leadership. The various interdenominational agencies of the nation are planning a long past due merger. There are seven of them. When they are joined into a single mighty interdenominational agency, a great step will be taken toward a united Church. To this national agency can be brought such problems as the providing of subsidies, supervision and help for the sparsely populated areas; the issue of housing; the provision of ministerial leadership for special situations such as the new community and the crowded student populations in the universities with large numbers of veterans. There are all kinds of issues of national and world concern to which the Church must reply with a united response. The impact and power of the Church must be brought to bear on the great economic and political and social questions that face the nation. There has been some accomplishment along this line but it is far from what it might be. If the Protestant denominations were willing to surrender more of their sovereignty, the national interdenominational agency could be made the true instrument through which the Church acts, leads, trains and obtains its leadership.

There are world economic and political issues that demand

a united Church even more than do problems at the national level. The World Council of Churches is demonstrating its capacity to get nations and groups to work together in feeding the hungry and in rehabilitating those orphaned by war. It is gratifying that many of our foreign missions are done on a united Church basis, but we have just made a beginning. We cannot hope to have one world unless we respond to the call of the True Church that its people become one in Christ.

The True Church asks not only for a more effective inter-denominational approach but it seeks leadership that will formulate ways by which a united Church may be achieved. Dr. Paul Payne of the Presbyterian church and Dr. E. Stanley Jones are both working—separately, but with something of the same idea—toward a plan for a united Church. Dr. Jones' idea is in terms of a federal union Church, patterned after our union of states. His would be a United Church of America, with each Protestant denomination member referred to as a branch— the Methodist branch of the United Church, the Presbyterian branch, the Disciples branch, the Episcopal branch. The theory is that the denominations would gradually surrender sovereignty in various areas, as they learned to carry on their basic work together.

Dr. Payne thinks in terms of getting church leaders together to draw up what he terms a "Charter of Union." When the charter has been perfected by the best thinking of those devoted to the idea of a united Church, it will be offered to the various denominations in much the same manner as nations were asked to accept the charter of the United Nations. As the denominations come together, Dr. Payne believes, they will begin to surrender sovereignty. They might, for example, join together in formulating one program for junior high school students, one program for the college age or for young adults, and in building up a common staff for that particular age group. Or they might join in publishing an outstanding paper for senior high school people. They might unite in building one outstanding seminary that would train ministers for the True Church, or in founding a great Protestant university. It is not difficult to sense the amazing possibilities that open before the surrendering of denominational sovereignty. It is that kind of leadership, that kind of vision, that kind of readiness to grow beyond the vested interest of the denominational institution, to which the True Church calls.

On a world basis there is a tremendous demand for new leadership. Never in history has there been as great a need to send out of America skilled leadership—leadership with the skill to heal the body, to illumine the mind, to guide the growth of the spirit, to rebuild the community, to direct public health, to distribute food, to revise and reorganize use of natural resources, to aid education, to strengthen the home, to renew the Church. There are resources in America for sending hundreds of young people, trained in Christian life and in discipline of the mind, to all corners of the earth. There are the resources, if there were the will. It remains only for individual Christians and for the Church to gird themselves and respond to the call of the world's needs.

There are two mighty alternatives before the world. They are Christianity and statism or, as someone has put it, "Christ or Chaos." If we continue to work separately either in the local community or on a national level, we will never be able to call forth the needed leadership; we will never be able to amass the resources. We are willing to send our young men all over the world to die on bloody battlefronts, but we are not willing to match their consecration with ambassadors of peace, with builders, with the conservers of life, with the bearers of the vision that will build the world of which men dream. In war we unite as one to kill; can we not then become one to build in peace? It is such a call that the True Church gives. It is such a challenge that the True Church makes to leadership.

III

The True Church calls for the enlistment and training of lay leadership to share creatively in its local ministry, and in county, state, national and world activities. The relationship between lay and professional leaders should be one of mutual inspiration. The spiritual growth that results from participation is at once the goal of the professional leader and the motivation of the lay participant.

Enlistment of lay leadership is closely related to the vitality of the Church's spiritual life. I take an illustration from my own church, where once it was almost impossible to get teachers for the church school and personnel for boards and committees. When I wanted the young people to share in the leadership of the morning service, I found them hesitant and reluctant. After more than ten years, the church school staff is complete, with a waiting list. Prior to the last annual meeting, when more than two hundred and fifty persons were asked to work on committees, boards, and in other capacities, only three persons declined. The reciprocal ministry of the church has become so vital and so central in the life of the community that its members believe in it, want to share in it, find meaning in being a part of it. Having received fully, they give freely.

The ten years have been marked by spiritual growth in individual lives, in the fellowship of the church, and in the relation of the church to the community as a whole. To the ministerial staff, they have been years of rich experience. Hundreds of couples have been guided prior to marriage and in the years since have been helped in the building of their homes. Parents in several thousand families have found the church to be a rich resource for their children and young people. Individuals have been guided in their choice of vocations and in getting jobs. Men have been helped to go into their own businesses. Many have been helped through crises. Friendless persons have been helped to know friendship; childless couples have been assisted in adopting children; scores have been led out of emotional confusion into health of mind and soul. Hundreds have been helped in winning freedom for growth and other hundreds have been kept free to grow. Families facing disintegration have been helped to grow into real units of God's Kingdom. Scores of persons have been guided through sorrow to the rare experience of being "more than conquerors." In the church, its camps and its extensive outreaches, young people have come to realize that the vitality and joy they have known has been within the church rather than in secular fellowships.

It is out of participation in such ministries and in the sharing of such fellowships that persons grow into a readiness to give themselves to training and leading. They are the first step the True Church must take toward the enlistment of lay leadership.

The second step involves the reality of lay participation. Professional leadership must get its satisfaction out of the growth of lay leaders. It never does what the lay staff can and will do, for lay persons of fine abilities will only participate if their functions are clear and real. Decompensated persons may be willing to serve as figure heads, but individuals of intelligence and stature can be led to consecration only where the work is worthy of their self-dedication. The jobs assigned them must be significant, the resources must be available, the methods clear, the chances for training must be provided. And out of their participation must come a continuous motivation for spiritual growth.

At first, the staff must perform many of the functions of leadership. Ten years ago in my own church, the minister planned and directed the program of education in giving and the annual canvass. Today it is planned and carried out completely by laymen. At first the minister planned the summer camps and provided most of the leadership in camp play, worship and other program activities. Now the camps are directed and run by those who were once campers. Once the minister did all of the calling on prospective members; now calling is done exclusively by lay members. While in the beginning the minister alone called on members, now deacons and members of the board of women make thousands of calls a year. While the minister once did all of the personal counseling, members now share in counseling activities that cover all aspects of living from preparation for marriage to comforting the bereaved. There was a time when the minister represented the church in all community and beyond-the-church activities; now scores of lay leaders share in all of these outreaches. Once I was the only minister; now there are three others with another soon to be added. In the beginning there was one full-time member of the staff and two part-time leaders. Now there are twenty-six full-time and twelve part-time members on the staff.

A third step in enlisting lay leaders is to guide the growth of the Church from the pulpit-centered program of a one-day Church to an all-inclusive ministry for a seven-day fellowship of growth and service. Leaders grow out of leading. If children sit and listen, they learn little. If they share and do, they learn and teach one another. If a staff member teaches a Bible class, he grows. But if he helps a lay member so that he may in turn teach, the layman grows. If the layman so guides the class that each member helps in the teaching, there is growth in all. Let two hundred men and women plan the new year's program and interpret it to the entire Church and the results are infinitely more significant than if the minister did it alone. Leaders may be born leaders, but they only grow by leading.

The True Church provides part-time payment for some of its lay leaders as departmental superintendents in the church school. These persons need to give extra time to train and supervise teachers and to program planning. But beyond this, lay leadership should operate on the principle of tithing of time.

Leadership training may be provided on four bases. The first is the best: training on the job, in the very process of leading and teaching. The basic resources of leadership should be supplied at the time the individual receives membership in the fellowship of the Church, and are augmented by personal supervision, programs of reading and special training before the person undertakes a given job. In one church, the board of deacons takes six months to train new deacons before they assume their active duties. In one church school, persons serve as assistant teachers before they become regular teachers, and departmental superintendents begin as teachers. Adult sponsors of youth work in this church are taken to camp and given instruction before they undertake their jobs.

A second form of training is given in departmental instruction before the year begins and at intervals during the year. Outsiders are invited to these courses of instruction to share their views. This training may be jointly led by minister, staff and officers of the department.

A third type of training is more general, provided by area training conferences where leaders of two or more churches join in training activities. In these conferences there is interchange of ideas among church leaders and pooling of resources to enlist outside leadership. Many of these conference-type schools are held throughout the country. There is need for many more, where there is less lecturing and more of the workshop type of activity.

The fourth kind of leadership training is of the more formal type provided by professional schools in short-term courses and by national agencies during the summer months. These opportunities provide for wide exchange of ideas between local, professional and lay leadership. These, too, need to grow in the direction of the workshop type of training. There now are a number of opportunities for workshop training in the use of radio, creative use of leisure and leadership of children and youth. The True Church asks that these workshops multiply all over the nation.

It is enlistment along the foregoing lines that will result in lay leaders going beyond the local church to assume community, state and national responsibilities. The need for a mighty lay movement in the Church, the nation and throughout the world, is long overdue. What Wesley did long ago, needs now to be done on a far greater basis and on all frontiers of the True Church's ministry.

IV

To realize the True Church as we have conceived it, with staff and lay leadership as here envisioned, vast resources will be needed. Such a program will cost heavily in effort, time and money. The contemporary Church gets all it deserves and can use effectively. But if we are to get richer returns, we must make bigger investment.

If the True Church is to be a redeeming force in the desperate plight of our secular world, it will take great dedication, the all-out efforts of the strongest leaders in the Christian vocations, a tithe of the time of all laymen, and a tithe plus an offering of the income of all. The cost will be small in comparison to the toll if it be not paid.

The True Church, we repeat as our final word, has both individual and collective aspects. In each person whose life fulfills the Divine purpose in all areas of living, the True Church is manifest. In a fellowship of two or more persons who seek with complete devotion to live by the will of God for the good of all men, and who seek to grow in union with God through individual and corporate worship, the True Church is revealed.

INDEX